WHO KILLED DANIEL MORGAN?

By

Paul Harris

Born in Wolverhampton, England in
1967, Paul Harris is the author of three novels
and one work of non-fiction. Much of his
earlier work was published in the small press
magazines of the 90's, including "Good Stories"
magazine in December 1994 and in
"Staple" magazine the following summer.

Cover Art by TJ Harris

ISBN-13: 978-1542304399
ISBN-10: 1542304393

Contents

Appendices

1

The Murder, the Motives and the "Flawed" Investigation

As one of Britain's most notorious unsolved murders the Daniel Morgan case dredges the murky depths of police corruption and touches the lives of some of our most prominent public figures. The Morgan family claim to have been the victims of cover-up after police cover-up. Even after 30 years and five police investigations, nobody has ever stood trial for the killing. The case has been the subject of television documentaries, parliamentary debates, and judicial inquiries and yet justice has still not been served.

The events surrounding the crime have been made deliberately confusing: smokescreens have been formed, documents have been misplaced, witnesses mishandled, and lines of inquiry left unpursued. The family's campaign for justice, however, holds firm to this day.

Their complex tale began on the evening of Tuesday 10th March 1987 when a group of men met for a drink in a pub in South London. The establishment in question was the Golden Lion in Sydenham, a place now irrevocably linked with the events of that particular evening.

The Golden Lion still sits on the busy Sydenham Road. It is now surrounded by discount stores and takeaway shops. A small beer garden runs parallel with the street. Dotted with greenery and foliage, it provides an oasis amongst the diesel fumes and the hurly-burly of urban life. To one side of the pub is a dimly lit cobbled access road that leads to garages and a blood-stained car park.

Among the group of drinkers on that particular evening were serving officers based at Catford police station, situated not ten minutes away along Southend Lane. Also present were two partners in a firm of private investigators. Their names were Jonathan Rees and Daniel Morgan. The name of their company was Southern Investigations, a name that was about to be launched into the national consciousness. Southern Investigations were to become the most notorious firm of investigators since the Pinkertons. The exact nature of their relationship with officers of the Metropolitan Police Service is yet another story that was to be very slowly unravelled. The events that followed would provide the catalyst for one of the biggest scandals in British journalistic history.

Daniel Morgan (Photo: REX)

The party broke up just before nine o'clock when Rees says that he left the Golden Lion to meet another business associate at another pub nearer to his home. Rees had left his car parked in the road at the front of the pub and, accordingly, left by the front door, weaving between the tables in the beer garden, before driving away.

Although their relationship had been tense of late and the partners had been seen arguing only the night before, Rees and Morgan cordially waved to one another as Rees made his departure. According to Rees, this was the last time he saw his business partner alive. As he left, he saw Morgan still sitting at the table making notes, as had become his custom of late.

Daniel sat for a little longer until he too left the Golden Lion. He had parked in the car park at the rear of the pub, and left by the back door. Exactly what happened next remains shrouded in mystery. What is known is that the next time anybody admits to seeing Daniel Morgan, he was lying in a pool of blood next to his BMW with the blade of an axe deeply embedded in his face and two packets of crisps lying beside him, one for each of his two young children.

Morgan had been assaulted with enormous savagery. He had been struck over and over again and with such force that the axe could not be removed from his head until the post-mortem, during which, it was noted by the examiner that the handle of the axe had been wrapped in sticking plaster to prevent the assailants hand from slipping during the attack, which strongly suggested that it had been unquestionably premeditated. The final blow to the victim's face was delivered as he lay on the car park dying from his wounds. This ensured that his final breath was extinguished before he could utter a word.

Daniel Morgan, who was 37 years old, was married with two children. He, along with his brother Alastair, had been born in Singapore to a British army officer who had fought at the Battle of Arnhem with the Parachute Regiment in 1944. When his father died prematurely, his mother Isobel remarried. It was Morgan's stepfather who would introduce Daniel to the murky world of private investigation, and in so doing inadvertently began the chain of events that would culminate in a pub car park in South London.

When Alastair Morgan first visited that car park,

shortly after his brother's murder, he recollects being struck by the lack of a customary police cordon and no apparent attempt at all by the police to preserve the integrity of the scene or the forensic evidence that it may have possessed. In fact, the forensic investigation was subsequently described as *"pathetic"* by a Hampshire Police review of the case.

When the body was discovered, Morgan's watch was missing, presumably stolen. Curiously though, his wallet containing credit cards and over £1,000 in cash had not been touched by the would-be thief. Even more curious was the fact that one of Daniel's pockets had been ripped open. The notes that he had spent most of the evening compiling were never found. It is alleged that a DNA trace was found on the torn pocket but was never fully investigated.

In the days following the murder, rumour and speculation were rife. Theories regarding a possible motive were plentiful. Morgan had a reputation as a notorious womaniser and it was suggested that a jealous husband may have tracked him down and exacted his revenge; that Morgan may have dabbled with the wrong woman. Another theory was that a disgruntled client had sought him out and attacked him. Much of Morgan's work had been as a bailiff and a debt collector. Enemies were in no short supply.

Possibly the most intriguing hypothesis was outlined by authors Michael Gillard and Laurie Flynn in their definitive 2004 book about police corruption, *The Untouchables*.

A year before his death, Daniel Morgan had been retained by the BBC's legal department to source evidence that could be used to defend a libel case that was being brought against them by high ranking Conservative Party members including Neil Hamilton, and funded by billionaire James Goldsmith.

The BBC's *Panorama* had aired a documentary investigating the existence of right wing extremism within the Tory ranks. The programme was called

"Maggie's Militant Tendency" and alleged, amongst other things, that during a visit to Berlin, Hamilton had been seen goose-stepping and giving Nazi salutes. It is thought that Morgan's involvement in this affair may have brought him to the attention of MI5 and other agencies working on behalf of the government and the Conservative Party. Indeed, it was at this time that Morgan had both his car and his offices broken into.

The murder scene in the car park of the Golden Lion with Morgan's blood still in the foreground

However, the most enduring motive is that Morgan was preparing to expose massive police corruption in the Met. Whether the specific details involved the trafficking of huge amounts of drugs and the laundering of the proceeds from that trade through Southern Investigations, as has been suggested by Stephen Wright in the *Daily Mail,* or whether it was the illegal, and very lucrative, trade in confidential police information through Southern Investigations to its clients on Fleet Street, we will probably never know.

Former Metropolitan Police Assistant Commissioner John Yates wrote in the *Independent* some years later that Morgan was about to *"expose serious corruption and drug-dealing between police and private investigators."*

It is known that Southern Investigations had connections with both Clifford Norris, a kingpin of the South London drugs trade at the time, and multi-millionaire gangland boss Kenneth Noye. Morgan is said to have disapproved of the direction in which his partner, Rees, was steering their firm. His brother claims that he complained to him about it only weeks before his death, saying: *"They are all over the place down here."*

One of the men who were later arrested for his murder was alleged to have told a fellow inmate whilst he was on remand that Daniel was killed because he *"knew too much"*.

Certainly, at the coroner's inquest into Daniel's death, Detective Chief Superintendent Douglas Campbell, who was in charge of the murder investigation admitted that there was a strong suggestion that Morgan had a story to sell and that the figure being bandied about was a huge £250,000. If this figure was correct it would have had to have been an incredible story with major implications. Campbell added that he had found *"no evidence at all"* that this story existed. In fact, it is believed that the figure involved was a much more modest £40,000, and that the reporter involved was Alex Marunchak of the *News of the World.*

Marunchak, himself, has always insisted that he never met Morgan and had no knowledge of him prior to his death, a claim that has been brought into serious doubt by the testimony of Bryan Madagan, a retired private investigator, who once employed both Morgan and Rees. Regardless of whether Marunchak was telling the truth or not, it appears that he was not initially interviewed by detectives and asked about the story relating to police corruption that Morgan was allegedly preparing to sell him.

Ukrainian-born Marunchak who, at the time, was also employed as a Scotland Yard interpreter with access to sensitive information, later became an executive editor on the *News of the World* under the editorship of Andy Coulson, and a close associate of News International chairman Rupert Murdoch. Coulson later became director of communications for the then Prime Minister David Cameron until his ignominious resignation from the post amidst the phone-hacking scandal. Another victim of that very public scandal was Mr Marunchak himself who, along with another man, was arrested in 2012 on suspicion of committing criminal breaches of privacy. The name of Marunchak's co-conspirator was Jonathan Rees of Southern Investigations. Charges were not brought and the two men were released when the Crown Prosecution Service concluded that the Met had taken too long to investigate the allegations against them.

Back in 1987, the unfortunate Mr Rees had once more attracted the attention of the police. He was dragged from his home in the middle of the night to be informed of the brutal murder of his, now former, business partner Daniel Morgan. He was asked by the attendant police officers to accompany them to the police station for questioning. It also fell to Rees to formally identify the body. Apparently this was in order to spare Morgan's family such a traumatic experience.

It should be pointed out, quite clearly, that Jonathan Rees has always, and quite consistently, denied any involvement in Daniel's death. Indeed, as recently as 2014, he still claimed that overwhelming police interest in him had hindered the investigation from the start. Unfortunately for Rees though his proximity to the deceased only moments before the attack, not to mention their increasingly volatile relationship, made him an automatic suspect.

To compound his problems further, it was known that Rees and Morgan had fallen out over an incident some months earlier. Unknown to Morgan, Rees had agreed to supervise the transfer of a large amount of cash on behalf of Belmont Car Auctions. The two security guards that Rees had hired were his brothers-in-law, Glenn and Garry Vian. Their task was to collect £18,000 in cash and deposit it in a night safe at the Midland Bank. According to Rees, the three men arrived at the bank only to find that the safe had been "super-glued shut". Seemingly unperturbed by this, Rees decided to drop the other two men home and take the cash to his house for safe-keeping. As he walked from his car, Rees says that he was attacked from behind by two unidentified assailants who sprayed ammonia in his face and robbed him of the money.

But Rees didn't seek medical attention and Daniel Morgan didn't believe his story. He accused him of stealing the money himself. So did the proprietors of Belmont Car Auctions who promptly initiated legal proceedings against Southern Investigations. Morgan was livid. Southern weren't insured for carrying large amounts of cash and he feared that this loss could mean their ruination.

On the night he died, Morgan had been invited to the Golden Lion by Rees to discuss the loss and the possibility of securing funds to pay for it. They were to meet a man by the name of Paul Goodridge who would be able to arrange the money.

It is known that Morgan was reluctant to deal with Goodridge and had to be persuaded by Rees to attend the Golden Lion that night. It was later claimed that Rees needed the meeting to take place in the jurisdiction of Catford police station, which the Golden Lion is.

Goodridge was a violent criminal; a bodyguard, a henchman, and a possible underworld hit-man. But he never turned up to the meeting with Rees and Morgan and his exact whereabouts on that night remain unclear.

Prior to his proposed meeting with Rees and Goodridge, Morgan firstly went to see an Estate Agent called Margaret Harrison with whom he'd being having an affair. They had a drink and then Morgan left for his meeting to discuss funding the missing money.

The Golden Lion public house on Sydenham Road
(Photo: Enterprise Inns)

The investigating officer in the Belmont Car Auctions robbery case had been a Detective Constable Duncan Hanrahan who happened to be the duty officer on the night that Rees reported the robbery. It is claimed that Hanrahan's investigation was less than thorough and that he failed to question key witnesses. It appears that he too doubted Rees's story. In fact, he went so far as to suggest this in his written report of the robbery when he noted that "*to attack somebody outside their house and get away with £18,000, you would have to be the luckiest mugger in the world.*"

Interestingly, Hanrahan, an associate of Rees's who was also known to drink in the Golden Lion, was shortly to become part of the investigative team into Daniel Morgan's murder. It was he who testified against Rees at the 1988 inquest into Morgan's death. He claimed that Rees had told him that he was intending to soil the reputation of the leading officers involved in bringing Morgan's killer to justice. He named Detective Chief Superintendent Campbell and Detective Inspector Alan Jones as his targets and discussed planting drugs in Jones's car. He also made plans to spread malicious gossip about Jones regarding an extra-marital affair. Although Hanrahan himself was later jailed on corruption charges, this all weighed heavily against Jonathan Rees's claims of innocence.

As the police investigation into Morgan's death gained momentum Rees was initially questioned by Detective Sergeant Sid Fillery at Catford police station. Fillery himself presents a hugely interesting character. Described by some as "*an extremely unpleasant man*" and by others as a drunk, he had a reputation for corruption and for framing people he didn't like. As if these characteristics weren't endearing enough, he also had a predilection for child pornography. It is even claimed that he kept a stash of such material in his office, an allegation given more credence by his arrest in August 2003. He was later charged with, and convicted for, making indecent images of children.

But in 1987 Fillery was a senior detective and found himself assigned to the Daniel Morgan murder case. It may be pertinent, at this point, to inquire of the whereabouts of DS Fillery during the hours leading up to Morgan's brutal murder. Astonishingly, the night before the killing, he had been present in the Golden Lion public house in Sydenham, just minutes from Catford police station. He was there having a drink with his very close personal friend, Jonathan Rees, for whom he had been moonlighting in contravention of police regulations.

Daniel Morgan was also there, as were several of Fillery's colleagues from the Met, and a handful of career criminals who also held close ties with Southern Investigations. During the evening, an altercation broke out and some pushing and shoving ensued. Morgan was at the centre of the dispute and, shortly afterwards, left under a cloud, only to be persuaded to return to the scene the following evening.

The Morgan family's thirty year campaign for justice has been thwarted not by the involvement of the *News of the World* in 2002 or by events at the Old Bailey in 2010, but by what happened at Catford CID on 11th March 1987, the day after Daniel's death. This was, namely, Detective Sergeant Fillery's involvement in the initial stages of the first investigation and his subsequent mishandling, deliberate or otherwise, of the case, the evidence, and the witnesses.

So why was Fillery investigating the case at all? He was a known associate and very close friend of the prime suspect. He may, or may not, have even been at the scene of the crime very shortly before it was committed. How does it fall that a man with such close ties to a murder case is secured as the investigating officer?

Fillery interviewed Rees on the day after Daniel Morgan's death. He ordered no forensic examination of Rees's clothes or of his car. Instead, he told his friend that he could pop the clothes that he had been wearing the previous evening into the station at his convenience the following day. This curiously relaxed approach to a murder suspect also meant that Rees was able to visit the offices of Southern Investigations; premises that Fillery had declined to secure for the investigation; and remove files in a black bin liner.

The file relating to Belmont Car Auctions and the

work that Southern Investigations had undertaken for them, some of which involved moonlighting officers from Catford police station, was never subsequently recovered by the police. Also missing was Daniel's 1987 desk diary which he was known to diligently keep up to date. It is unclear whether these items, both representing crucial evidence in the case, were taken away by Rees on this visit or whether they were removed later when DS Fillery finally conducted an official search of the offices. Either way, neither the Belmont Car Auctions file nor the diary were ever logged by the police and were never made available for use as evidence in Morgan's murder case.

Fillery only remained on the case for four days but this was long enough for him to seriously undermine any potential prosecution of Rees, or anybody else, for his partner's murder. His lack of protocol was so blatant that his superiors began to suspect that he was deliberately sabotaging the case. Detective Chief Superintendent Campbell, the officer in charge of the investigation, went as far as accusing Fillery of *"ripping the guts out of the case."*

The following year, at the inquest into Morgan's death, Fillery claimed that he stepped aside as soon as he realised that there may have been a conflict of interests. This is a claim that Campbell strongly refutes. He was said to be *"furious"* when he discovered Fillery's relationship with the suspect, and personally had Fillery removed from the case.

Indeed, Campbell was so furious that he had Fillery arrested for perverting the course of justice along with two more officers from Catford who he suspected of being involved with the Belmont Car Auctions security operation. They were PC Peter Foley and PC Alan Purvis. Rees and his brothers-in-law, Glenn and Garry Vian were also arrested on suspicion of murder. All six were later released without charge due to a lack of evidence. Foley and Purvis were to later receive compensation for wrongful arrest.

The front page of the *Sun*, April 12th 1988

Rees still claims that after Fillery was removed from the case, his treatment at the hands of the police became more hostile and that the ongoing investigations and the incompetence with which they were conducted have blighted his life for more than a quarter of a century. This feeling of antipathy may have been why he told Duncan Hanrahan that he intended to harm Campbell and DI Jones's reputations.

Two days after his brother's murder, Alastair Morgan visited Catford police station to speak to detectives about a suspicion he held regarding Daniel's death. He told them that he was convinced that the murder was linked to the Belmont Car Auctions robbery and that Daniel had information about it that had resulted in his being killed. The detective whom Alastair spoke to was Detective Sergeant Sid Fillery. Of course, he had no idea that Fillery was such a close personal friend of the man whom he was attempting to implicate in his brother's murder.

Alastair explained his theory to Fillery and the connection to the robbery, but was surprised when Fillery simply responded by asking, *"What robbery was that then?"* Fillery denies any knowledge of this conversation ever taking place.

By the time the inquest into Daniel Morgan's death took place, in April 1988, at Southwark Coroner's Court, Fillery had retired from the force on medical grounds and had taken a full police pension. Remarkably, instead of disappearing quietly into the shadows, he took a job at Southern Investigation, replacing the deceased Daniel Morgan as Jonathan Rees's new partner.

The presiding coroner at the inquest was Sir Montague Levine who was later described, in his own 2013 obituary as *"Britain's most colourful coroner."* A larger than life character, Levine sported a handlebar moustache, wore a fresh rose or carnation in his buttonhole every day, and had a passion for vintage Jaguar cars. Throughout his career as a South London coroner, he was a strong advocate of rule 43 under which a coroner was allowed to *"make recommendations to prevent another death happening in similar circumstances."* Among his many controversial statements, he once criticised an American evangelist called Dr Morris Cerullo when an epileptic woman died after she stopped taking her tablets because she thought that she had been cured at a religious rally.

Nine years after the Morgan Inquest, Sir Montague would preside over the inquest into Stephen Lawrence's 1993 murder in Eltham, southeast London where he would be met with a *"wall of silence"* from Jamie Acourt and his gang. With characteristic forthrightness, the eminent coroner summed up the Lawrence case by telling the inquest jury: *"What we have established is that a group of cowardly white youths killed a young man for no other reason than that he was black."* The jury ruled that Stephen had been unlawfully killed in *"a completely unprovoked attack by five white youths"*.

The 1988 Daniel Morgan Inquest itself was no less explosive. Kevin Lennon worked for Southern Investigations. Routinely described as company secretary, accountant, and book keeper, his testimony stole the show. Lennon claimed that Rees had asked him on at least two separate occasions to find someone to kill Daniel Morgan. He told Levine, *"He was of the impression that I knew people who could or would be willing to kill Morgan."*

"He asked me this on at least two occasions. On each occasion I attempted to dissuade Rees from considering such a course of action. He was adamant that he wanted Morgan killed."

He went on to describe a conversation which, he says, took place at the Victory pub in Thornton Heath, during the course of which, Lennon alleges that Rees told him not to worry about arranging Morgan's death and that he had got it *"fixed"*. Rees allegedly explained to Lennon that he had friends at Catford police station who were willing to do it for him. He had also told Lennon that he had a new business partner in mind once Morgan was out of the way: Sid Fillery. Fillery was to take a medical retirement and join Rees at Southern Investigations.

It was, in fact, Kevin Lennon's testimony that first revealed that Sid Fillery was indeed now working with Rees at Southern Investigations. Lennon also told the court that Rees had discussed the murder with his wife Sharon, sister of Garry and Glenn Vian.

When Sharon Rees was called to give evidence, she sent a note to the coroner saying that she was too ill to attend. The next day, Daily Mirror reporter Sylvia Jones photographed Mrs Rees whilst out shopping.

Sid Fillery after being acquitted of involvement in Daniel Morgan's murder in 2010 (Photo: PA)

The inquest heard from various witnesses who alleged that Detective Sergeant Fillery had tampered with evidence during the investigation into Daniel Morgan's murder and had attempted to interfere with witnesses. Detective Chief Superintendent Douglas Campbell admitted that Fillery's involvement in the case may have compromised any possibility of making a conviction. Rees categorically denied playing any part in his partner's death.

These sensational claims sent shock waves down Fleet Street, and the press had a field day. Lennon's testimony was liberally splashed across the front pages. Huge amounts of newsprint were dedicated to the story by publications such as *The Sun, The Times,* the *Daily Mirror,* the *Daily Mail,* and the *Evening Standard.*

The *News of the World,* however, remained unusually tight lipped just as they had done over Daniel Morgan's death and subsequent investigation the previous spring. This was despite one of their senior crime reporters being present at the inquest. Throughout the story of Daniel Morgan's death, from start to finish, Alex Marunchak's name keeps springing up.

To adequately record Marunchak's association with the Morgan case and his alleged involvement in police corruption over a period of many years would take a book on the scale of *"War and Peace".* It was he who was allegedly involved in the £250,000 purchase of Morgan's story about police corruption. Authors Gillard and Flynn interviewed disgraced cop Sid Fillery for *The Untouchables.* During the course of which interview, Fillery told them that Marunchak had been one of Southern Investigations' key contacts and had even, on occasion, joined himself and Jonathan Rees at the Victory in Thornton Heath to discuss business.

It was through their association with Alex Marunchak that Southern Investigations were introduced to the infamous *News of the World* investigative reporter, Mazher Mahmood. Mahmood was a master of Fleet Street's "dark arts" and a practitioner of the worst kind of tabloid journalism. In 2005, Mahmood published a story in the *News of the World* about an eighteen-year-old mother who agreed to sell her young daughter to him for a reputed £15,000. Mahmood recorded a meeting between himself, the woman and her boyfriend during which the couple demonstrated no concern at all for the fate of their daughter. At the time Andy Coulson, then editor of the newspaper, claimed that Mahmood's investigation had saved the child's life.

However, later that year, Florim Gashi, a close associate of Mahmood's and one of his paid informants, gave an interview to Roy Greenslade of *The Guardian* in which he claimed: *"I got her boyfriend to persuade her to do it. She didn't know what was happening. She was a good mother and I regret being involved."* Gashi also discredited the tape recording that Mahmood had made of their meeting, when he alleged that it had been edited in order to incriminate the young woman.

"Fake Sheik" Mazher Mahmood was finally jailed for perverting the course of justice in October 2016

Gashi had worked with Mahmood on a regular basis. In 2002 Mahmood "exposed" a plot to kidnap footballer David Beckham's wife, Victoria. Mahmood contacted the police but would provide neither the names of the kidnap gang or their intended target, so giving himself time to publish the story before the suspects were arrested. It appears that the Met were quite compliant with this arrangement. The gang were arrested and subsequently charged. The case against them, however, collapsed when it was revealed that Florim Gashi was the main prosecution witness and had been paid £10,000 by Mahmood for the story, most of which Gashi had fabricated with the sole intention of selling it to Mahmood.

On the 5th October 2016, Mazher Mahmood was finally convicted of conspiring to pervert the course of justice in relation to the doctoring of evidence in another fabricated story and subsequent court case about pop star and X-factor judge Tulisa Contostavlos. His driver, Alan Smith, was also found guilty of the same charge. During the course of the trial John Kelsey-Fry QC told jurors: "*Mr Mahmood is not a policeman. He is a journalist... securing convictions is not actually his job.*" Following his conviction it was thought that up to 18 victims of Mahmood's so-called "stings" were planning to launch civil claims against him, totalling around £800 million. Later that month, Mahmood was sentenced to 15 months at the Old Bailey by Judge Gerald Gordon. Lawyer Mark Lewis commented: "*Over the last 25 years, innumerable lives have been ruined by the dishonest actions of Mazher Mahmood. People have lost their livelihoods, their homes and relationships, with some spending time in prison.*"

It was during one of Mahmood's so-called sting operations that Sid Fillery claims to have dressed up as a secretary whilst Mahmood, himself, adopted his familiar role as the "fake sheik".

In 1992, Southern Investigations became involved in a plot by the media to expose the then Liberal Democrat leader Paddy Ashdown's five year-old affair with a House of Commons secretary called Patricia Howard. It had become common knowledge that documents relating to divorce proceedings and referring to the affair had been stolen from the offices of Ashdown's solicitor and were being touted around Fleet Street. Rees and Fillery were instructed by Alex Marunchak to obtain the documents on behalf of the *News of the World*.

They never did though. Present at the discussions relating to the Ashdown document was a corrupt detective by the name of Duncan Hanrahan. The very same Duncan Hanrahan who had led the investigation into the Belmont Car Auctions robbery and had later testified at the Daniel Morgan inquest. The same Duncan Hanrahan who was later jailed in 1999 for eight years for attempting to bribe a member of Scotland Yard's ant-corruption team. Hanrahan had a grudge against Marunchak and tipped off City of London police who made the rendezvous instead of Southern Investigations.

After Hanrahan's arrest in 1997, he himself became a police informant and claimed that he had worked with over 50 fellow officers who were corrupt. He also alleged that he had been told by one of these officers that Daniel Morgan had been killed to prevent him exposing corrupt police practises. It is also believed that Hanrahan named Commander Ray Adams of Scotland Yard as one of these corrupt officers. It is thought that it was Hanrahan's evidence that prompted then Metropolitan Police Commissioner Paul Condon to make his controversial October 1997 statement in which he declared that there were about 250 corrupt officers currently serving in the Metropolitan Police Service.

Commissioner Condon made a further statement in December the same year: "*I honestly believe I command the most honourable large city police service in the world. I believe that the overwhelming majority of the 27,000 men and women in the Met are honest, they are decent, they are brave... However, I do have a minority of officers who are corrupt, dishonest, unethical... They commit crimes, they neutralise evidence in important cases and they betray police operations and techniques to criminals. These bad officers sap the morale of their honest colleagues and they do immense damage to public confidence... they are very difficult to target and prosecute.*"

Paddy Ashdown, now Lord Ashdown, was a former Royal Marine and Special Boat Service officer. He remained as leader of the Liberal Democrats until his retirement in 1999, the same year incidentally as Hanrahan's imprisonment. He came out of the scandal relatively unscathed. Initially, he had applied for an injunction, banning publication of the story about his affair but, after some consideration, released the story himself, leading to the *Sun's* infamous headline, *"Paddy Pantsdown"*. His wife, Jane, forgave him and their thirty year marriage weathered the media storm.

2

Brinks Mat, Stephen Lawrence and the Gathering Stench of Corruption

Although Alex Marunchak was reported to have been seen at the inquest into Daniel Morgan's death, and to have been present there with none other than his friend, and the prime suspect in the case, Jonathan Rees who was now being paid substantial amounts of money by the *News of the World* for his dubious services, he reported not one word of the proceedings, just as he had declined to put pen to paper regarding the Morgan case at all. This despite him being one of his newspaper's leading crime correspondents. It was not as if he had no interest in such matters, as evidenced by his aggressive pursuit of other stories relating to police corruption.

Indeed, one of the stories that he did report on with some degree of zeal was that of Alan "Taffy" Holmes. Holmes was a Detective Constable who had been working on the investigation into the Brinks Mat gold bullion heist in November 1983. By 1987 an internal investigation into police corruption was well under way. Both Commander Ray Adams, head of Criminal Intelligence, and Detective Constable Holmes were to be interviewed regarding their suspected involvement with known criminal Kenneth Noye. Holmes and Adams were not only police colleagues but close friends and golfing partners. They also belonged to the same masonic lodge as Noye.

A colleague of Holmes on the Brinks Mat investigation spoke to Gillard and Flynn relating a comment Holmes had once made that had left a lasting impression on him. Holmes, looking uncharacteristically anxious had said to him: *"don't you ever take a penny from the likes of Kenneth Noye."* The officer believed that Holmes had been speaking from experience.

Although, there was never any evidence linking

28

Noye to the Brinks Mat robbery itself, police had strong reason to believe that he was playing a major role in disposing of the huge amounts of gold bullion that had been stolen and in July 1986, he was convicted of fencing some of the gold, serving eight years in prison.

During the investigation into Noye's involvement with the Brinks Mat gold, his isolated mansion in West Kingsdown in Kent was put under increasingly tight surveillance. One night in January 1985, Noye heard his dogs barking and went to investigate. When he found an intruder cornered by his three Rottweilers, an altercation broke out. The intruder was an undercover Detective Constable called John Fordham. Fordham was viciously stabbed more than ten times by Noye and died from his wounds shortly afterwards. Noye was subsequently found not guilty of the murder of the surveillance officer on the grounds of self-defence. He had claimed in court that he had believed himself to be under attack by an assassin sent by a rival underworld villain.

Also at Noye's house that night was a South London crook called Brian Reader. He managed to successfully flee the scene of Noye's struggle with DC Fordham but nevertheless he too was later convicted of handling gold bullion from the Brinks Mat raid and was consequently sentenced to nine years in prison.

In the book, *One Last Job,* published by Mirror Books in September 2016, journalists Tom Pettifor and Nick Sommerlad describe how Reader and his gang once came across photographs of a prominent Conservative cabinet minister abusing children whilst they were ransacking safety deposit boxes during a 1971 raid on Lloyd's Bank in Baker Street. They claim that the robbers were so sickened by the vile images that they left them scattered across the floor of the vault for the police to find, hoping that this would lead to the politician being brought to justice. He never was. The bank staff refused to co-operate with detectives investigating the robbery, insisting that the privacy of their clients was of paramount importance. Official documents from the time even go as far as to suggest that there ensued a *"heated argument"* between the two parties inside the vault itself. Bank officials declined to reveal the identities of safety deposit box holders or details of their visits to the vault. They also refused to allow the police to take property from the vault as evidence. The police were never made aware of the photographs that Brian Reader and his gang had left for them to find.

In March 2016, Reader was sentenced to six years at Woolwich Crown Court for his part in master-minding the £14 million Hatton Garden jewel robbery. Reader and his gang had tunnelled into the vault at Hatton Garden just as they had tunnelled into the Lloyd's Bank vault at Baker Street some 44 years previously. It has been said that the 76 year old pensioner caught the bus to Hatton Garden on the day of the heist using his free bus pass.

Kenneth Noye is currently serving life imprisonment for the shocking 1996 road rage murder of 21 year-old Stephen Cameron on an M25 slip road. Ironically, it wasn't his life of lucrative, and at times appallingly violent, crime that proved to be his undoing. Instead, it was his notoriously short temper.

Whilst driving a car that had been provided for him by south London car dealer John Marshall, Noye found himself being cut up by a van on a roundabout connecting the M25 and the M20. As both vehicles stopped at a set of traffic lights the incensed Noye leapt from his car and proceeded to confront the driver of the van. Stephen Cameron emerged from the van and stood his ground. As the pair began to brawl in the middle of the road, Cameron began to gain an advantage over the much older Noye. Further angered by what he saw as an unbearable humiliation, Noye returned to his car, armed himself with the knife that he routinely had about his person and twice stabbed Cameron in the chest with it. Noye nonchalantly drove away from the scene, leaving his victim to bleed to death in the arms of his fiancée, Danielle Cable.

The senseless killing sparked a huge manhunt as Noye escaped the country in a helicopter and headed for Spain. According to *The Independent* such was the concern over Noye's alleged ties to a network of corrupt serving Metropolitan Police officers that during the investigation into Cameron's murder, investigating officers were given around-the-clock protection from their own colleagues. Some were forced to change their telephone numbers and access to the case file was restricted to less than a dozen senior officers.

As if to emphasise the point, whilst Noye was on the run, Detective Constable John Donald was convicted of passing confidential police information to him, and so assisting him to elude capture. Donald was sentenced to 11 years for corruption.

Noye was finally arrested and extradited from Spain after Cameron's girlfriend Danielle Cable was flown out by police and was able to identify him as the killer. Despite being provided with a new identity under the witness protection programme, Cable was to find herself the subject of a £300,000 bounty placed on her head by Noye following his conviction in April 2000. Another witness who had testified against him in the case had already been found shot to death in his car in Kent. He had been murdered in broad daylight.

It later emerged that following Noye's abscondence, and prior to his extradition from Spain, a number of his former associates were also killed. Firstly, car dealer John Marshall was found shot dead in his Range Rover only days after Noye fled to the Continent. Police suspected that Noye had ordered the hit so that Marshall wouldn't be able to link the car that Noye was driving on the day of Cameron's death to Noye. Marshall had provided Noye with false documentation for the car and police were about to interview him in relation to this.

Keith Hedley had been a close friend of Noye's until the pair fell out over money. He was found shot dead on his yacht in Corfu shortly after Noye was believed to have visited the island whilst on the run.

Noye was also linked to the murder of Daniel Roff who was shot dead whilst sitting at the wheel of his car outside his home in Bromley. Roff was suspected by police of being the look-out during the assassination in Marbella of Great Train Robber Charlie Wilson. Wilson was said to have been shot dead along with his pet dog after he lost £3million of Brinks Mat money on a bungled drugs deal. Legend has it that, following Wilson's murder, his young British assassin calmly pedalled away into the bright Spanish sunshine on a yellow bicycle. He was never caught.

In September 2015 Kenny Noye was still serving a life sentence for the murder of Stephen Cameron and applied to be transferred to an open prison. The parole board made a recommendation in his favour, describing one of Britain's wealthiest, most powerful, most dangerous, and most violent criminals as having *"made considerable progress during his sentence into changing his attitudes."* Secretary of State Michael Gove disagreed and dismissed Noye's application.

In the eighties Detective Constable Alan "Taffy" Holmes had been a known associate of Kenneth Noye's and, according to *Daily Mail* reporter, Wensley Clarkson, so too was Daniel Morgan.

The operation investigating corruption between officers of the Metropolitan Police Service and Noye was called Operation Russell and in 1987 Holmes was interviewed by them twice. Shortly after the second interview, and on the eve of Commander Ray Adams being, himself, questioned about corruption, "Taffy" Holmes was found dead from shotgun wounds that were, apparently, self-inflicted.

Although there has been some speculation as to whether it would have been possible for Holmes to point the barrel of the shotgun at his own head and pull the trigger unaided, a suicide note was found at the scene in which Holmes blamed a fellow officer for driving him to his death. Holmes had suspected that this officer had been recording their conversations and passing them onto Operation Russell as part of the investigation into Ray Adams. It is this same officer who was later (anonymously) credited with seeing Holmes meeting with Daniel Morgan and Alex Marunchak in the weeks leading up to Morgan's death.

Many of those who, unwittingly or otherwise, crossed Kenneth Noye whilst he was at the height of his powers in the nineteen-eighties were later to be found dead or to have disappeared altogether. It is this that begs the question: were Daniel Morgan and Alan "Taffy" Holmes attempting to sell a story to Alex Marunchak about Noye's allegedly corrupt relationship with some of Scotland Yard's most senior officers? Were they about to expose the particular connection between officers on the ongoing Brinks Mat investigation and the leading suspects in the case?

According to Derek Haslam, a former fellow CID Detective, Holmes told him during an Indian meal that the two friends shared with Daniel Morgan in Thornton Heath in 1987 that he and Morgan had a huge story that they were about to sell to the press. They were asking £250,000 for the story. Haslam says that he did not see the relevance of this information until after Morgan's death, when he immediately informed the officer in charge of the murder investigation, Detective Chief Superintendent Douglas Campbell.

Referring to the deaths of both Daniel Morgan and Alan Holmes, Haslam later told Gillard and Flynn *"Those who kept the two deaths separate never wanted to know the truth"*.

Haslam also claims that ten years after their deaths, he was told by another officer that both the dead men had been seen meeting with *News of the World* crime reporter, Alex Marunchak; the same

Alex Marunchak who denied ever having heard of Morgan until after his death.

NEWS OF THE WORLD, August 2, 1987

COP KILLED HIMSELF TO SAVE PALS IN THE MASONS

Bribe probe row

COP killer Kenneth Noye has been blamed by angry Scotland Yard men for the suicide of a fellow-officer.

They believe Detective Constable Alan "Taff" Holmes shot himself rather than inform on other Freemasons implicated by Noye in a drugs and bribery scandal.

The 44-year old detective—Master of a South London masonic lodge—was found dead by his wife in the garden of their home in Shirley, near Croydon, last week.

He left a note complaining bitterly about the tactics of Yard anti-corruption investigators.

Holmes, who was not under suspicion himself,

HOLMES: Chat was bugged

By ALEX MARUNCHAK and GERRY BROWN

He claimed he stabbed the officer in self-...

Alex Marunchak reports on the tragic death of Detective Constable Alan Holmes then, two weeks later, puts his own spin on the funeral arrangements

—Comfort for widow, then the other woman attends wake—

YARD THROW PARTY FOR SUICIDE COP'S LOVER

By ALEX MARUNCHAK

SENIOR policemen laid on an amazing party for the secret girlfriend of suicide cop Alan "Taff" Holmes after his funeral.

Top Scotland Yard men comforted Holmes's grieving widow Lee and her two sons at the service.

Then they invited villain's wife Jean Burgess to an unofficial wake at the dead cop's favourite pub.

Holmes, 44, a high-ranking Freemason, killed himself because he refused to inform on fellow-members in the force alleged to have been involved in a drugs and bribery scandal.

QUESTIONED

He feared Yard investigators would threaten to rob his family about his friendship with Mrs Burgess, the dead man said.

Villain's wife goes to secret booze-up

HOLMES: Yard threat

MRS BURGESS: In tears

Shortly after Alan Holmes's "suicide", Alex Marunchak passed on evidence about Commander Adams to officers serving on Operation Russell. His enthusiasm for the story was relentless. Holmes died on the 27th of July. On August 2nd which was the following Sunday and Marunchak's first opportunity, he ran a story about the dead officer's links to both Commander Ray Adams and Kenneth Noye, and their membership of the freemasons. Two weeks later, his full page article in the *News of the World* accused Holmes of having a secret affair. The report was timed to coincide with the funeral at which event, of course, Holmes's widow was present. According to Marunchak, so too was his mistress.

In a 2002 article for the *Guardian* newspaper, reporter Graeme McLagan asserted that Jonathan Rees had sold information regarding the fugitive Noye to Marunchak and that the two of them were recorded by anti-corruption officers discussing how much money the *News of the World* owed Southern Investigations. The figure quoted was £7,555. We do not know what the information concerning Noye contained, but the more pertinent question is: from where did Rees source that information?

Although a cloud of suspicion dogged Commander Ray Adams for most of his highly impressive police career, he was never disciplined and nothing was ever proven against him. Operation Russell came up empty. He claimed that Noye was one of his informants. He was asked how, in 1987, he could afford to live in a £450,000 mansion adjoining a Surrey golf course on a policeman's wage. In response, he claimed that his wife was independently wealthy.

When black teenager Stephen Lawrence was surrounded and then stabbed to death by a gang of racist thugs whilst waiting at a bus stop in Eltham, south-east London on the evening of April 22nd 1993, the subsequent murder investigation became the overall responsibility of the senior Metropolitan Police officer for the area. That man was Commander Ray Adams. Although Adams claims, and possibly with good cause, that he had very little to do with the actual investigation, it is the taint of corruption left by Operation Russell and Adams's self-confessed association with Kenneth Noye that leads Stephen's mother Doreen Lawrence to maintain, even now, that the investigation was compromised from the start.

One of the gang was David Norris, later convicted and jailed for the killing, but not until nearly twenty years later in January 2012. His father was a notorious London gangster called Clifford Norris who was described in police documents as being suspected of *"involvement in organised crime, including armed robbery, importation and supply of drugs and murder."* Through his business interests, Norris was well connected with Kenneth Noye and therefore, some have speculated, with Commander Ray Adams.

Adams, however, denies knowing Norris. He also denies ever having met Detective Sergeant John Davidson even though Davidson was a close personal friend and colleague of Alan "Taffy" Holmes as was Adams. Davidson also regularly went drinking with Holmes as did Adams. Along with Adams, Davidson even gave evidence at the inquest into Holmes's death where he spoke of Holmes being *"worried by events to do with the police but outside his normal work"* the meaning of which he has never been asked to fully explain.

It is a matter of conjecture as to whether Davidson's close bond with Alan Holmes ever brought him into contact with Daniel Morgan prior to his death. The same can also be said of Ray Adams. The 2014 Mark Ellison Review of the police handling of the Stephen Lawrence case was undertaken on behalf of Home Secretary Theresa May and found that John Davidson was thought to have been involved in not one but two flawed murder investigations: those of both Lawrence and Morgan.

His exact role in the 1987 Morgan inquiry has, as yet, never been substantiated.

His role, however, in the Stephen Lawrence investigation has been well documented. DS Davidson had a leading part to play in the early days of the inquiry, interviewing suspects, witnesses, and informants. It was during these early inquiries that local people poured forward to put names and faces to the gang that had killed Stephen. Although, at the time, the police claimed that they were facing a *"wall of silence"* from a community in fear of reprisals from the gang, nothing could have been further from the truth.

In the days following the killing, as many as twenty-six independent witnesses came forward and willingly provided police with the names of the gang members who had killed Stephen Lawrence. The address of two of the suspects, Neil and Jamie Acourt, had even been supplied. Far from being afraid, many local residents were sickened by the senseless loss of Stephen's life and were keen to see justice served.

Despite this wealth of information, not one suspect was apprehended until two weeks later, and then only following a public outcry over a perceived lack of police activity. Nelson Mandela even referred to the case during a state visit to London. By the time the first three gang members were arrested any forensic evidence there may have been had already been destroyed.

At the time of Stephen's death, Neil Acourt and David Norris were already under investigation for the stabbing of another youth called Stacey Benefield. Three days after Benefield identified David Norris as his attacker during an identity parade, he made the acquaintance of Norris's father, Clifford, who, together with one of his henchmen, approached Benefield and strongly suggested that he should withdraw his evidence against the younger Norris. For this Benefield was offered £2000 in cash. An internal police report later said of Clifford Norris that he was *"a corruptor of police officers and an intimidator of witnesses."*

Detective Sergeant John Davidson was a larger than life, some might say imposing figure, and a rather abrasive Scotsman. There are claims that some witnesses in the Lawrence case were put off testifying by his surly manner. During the 1999 McPherson Inquiry into the police handling of the case, Sir William McPherson himself was scathing of the incompetent and insensitive handling of the investigation by the police in general and particularly in the case of Davidson. The report criticised him for being *"abrasive, incompetent and giving 'unsatisfactory' evidence"*. McPherson stated that Davidson had only himself to blame if members of the public perceived he and certain of his colleagues as *"institutionally racist"*.

Doreen and Neville, parents of murdered teenager Stephen Lawrence, meet Nelson Mandela (Photo:PA)

It was also revealed that Davidson had consistently refused to accept that the attack was racially motivated. This despite eye witness reports that the phrase *"What? What, nigger?"* was delivered by a member of the gang during the assault. McPherson concluded that this steadfast denial of motive also led to the initial investigation being inappropriately handled. Davidson told the inquiry: *""I do not think in my own mind that this was a racist attack. I still refuse to recognise it, sir."*

The Met's own intelligence reports said of Davidson that he had *"no integrity as a police officer and [was] always....open to offers from any source if financially viable".*

Possibly the most damaging accusation made against Davidson came from a self-confessed former corrupt detective called Neil Putnam. Putnam, who had once been a colleague of Davidson's in the South East Regional Crime Squad, claimed that Davidson had once bragged about his links to Clifford Norris and suggested that Norris *"had been putting some work our way".* Putnam also claimed that Davidson had told him that he *"was looking after Norris".* Putnam understood that to mean that Davidson had compromised the Lawrence investigation. Davidson of course denies that he was ever in the pay of Clifford Norris and nothing has ever been proven against him. He took medical retirement from the police service in 1998, along with a full pension. These days he owns a bar in Menorca ironically called The Smugglers Bar. The stench of corruption still follows him though. Even eight years after his retirement in 2006 senior police officer John Yates, then head of anti-corruption at Scotland Yard, went on record at the BBC as saying, *"From all the evidence I've seen and the intelligence I've seen, I have no doubt he* [Davidson] *was corrupt".*

One man who does not deny his dubious relationship with Clifford Norris is former Detective Sergeant David Coles, once of the Flying Squad.

Clifford Norris was a key player in the South London drugs trade and, in the nineteen-eighties, was importing huge amounts of cannabis from overseas. By 1988, he was under covert surveillance by Customs and Excise officials. During the course of their operation undercover investigators reported to the Met that on no less than four occasions Norris was observed meeting with Detective Sergeant David Coles at *The Tiger's Head* public house in Chislehurst close to Norris's £600,000 mock-Tudor mansion. Packages were apparently exchanged and Coles was seen by officers to be using a calculator.

Coles later claimed that he was grooming Norris as an informant. Norris, for his part, does not deny that he knew Coles but remains adamant that he has never had any corrupt dealings with the police. *"We were doing so well,"* he told Mark Townsend in a 2006 interview he gave to *The Observer*, *"there was never any reason for me to give money to the police."* At the time Clifford Norris believed that he was untouchable.

In fact, he had good cause to believe that he was operating beyond the reach of the law. At the time of the Stephen Lawrence investigation, Norris had been "on the run" from the police for six years. He was suspected of being a murderer, a drugs smuggler, and an arms dealer. Yet he was able to parade around south-east London and Kent without fear of being apprehended. He even took the time to explain the situation to Stacey Benefield while he was dissuading him from testifying against his son. He told Benefield that he was on the run from the police but *"he was putting his face up front and nothing was happening."*

When Detective Superintendent Bill Mellish took command of the re-investigation into Stephen's murder in 1994, it wasn't long before it became clear to him that Clifford Norris was exerting a malign and unhealthy influence on the inquiry. Within three months Mellish had him in custody. Norris's six years as a fugitive from justice had come to a swift end. He was shortly to find himself serving an eight year prison sentence for drugs and firearms offences.

Some were not convinced of the innocence of the relationship between Clifford Norris and Detective Sergeant Coles. Sir William McPherson, during his inquiry into Stephen Lawrence's murder, described Coles's meetings with Norris as *"plainly highly suspect"*. McPherson also referred to Norris as an *"evil influence"* and that he played a *"very damaging"* role in preventing witnesses from coming forward. In the light of the connection between Norris and certain officers of the Met, it was also noted with some suspicion that his son David was the only suspect in the Lawrence case who was not at home in the early hours of 7th May 1993, when officers swooped to arrest them.

Because of his association with Norris, Detective Sergeant Coles was hauled before the Met's Disciplinary Board who demanded his resignation. Coles appealed and was allowed to remain in the police service on the reduced rank of Detective Constable.

Curiously, police records show that during Coles's disciplinary procedure, he *"was seconded by Commander Ray Adams to perform a review of surveillance operations"*. If this is true, it seems astonishing that an officer who was at the time under investigation for possible corruption, and was known to be associated with alleged criminals who were themselves the subject of surveillance operations, should be assigned duties of such *"a delicate and confidential nature"*. On being questioned about his relationship with Coles, Commander Adams told the McPherson Inquiry that he had never heard of him. The episode remains however another stain on the integrity of Commander Ray Adams.

In 2014, Coles was working as a railway ticket inspector when journalists from the *Daily Mail* caught up with him. He admitted to them that although he later regretted it he did know Clifford Norris at the time that David Norris and his gang murdered Stephen Lawrence. Given this confession, it now seems startling that during the 1996 trial of three of the suspects in the Lawrence case, Coles was one of the officers assigned to guard Duwayne Brooks, a key witness and the friend who was with Stephen on the night that he was fatally stabbed.

The case collapsed when Duwayne Brooks's eyewitness accounts were deemed unreliable. McPherson, commenting on Coles's role during the trial, said: *"Anybody who had known would have regarded him* [Coles] *as a wholly inappropriate person to guard Mr Brooks"*.

There is no hard evidence to suggest that either John Davidson or Ray Adams had links to Coles, nor was Coles directly involved in the Stephen Lawrence murder investigation. Adams, Davidson, and Coles have all since retired from the Met on full pensions.

The alleged killers of Stephen Lawrence are attacked by demonstrators following their appearance before the McPherson Inquiry (Photo:PA)

In 2005, Doreen Lawrence wrote to Alastair Morgan to express her understanding of the frustration she shared with him. She wrote: *"I sympathise with your family situation and all what you are going through since your brother's death. What is so unbelievable is the level of corruption that existed in the police force then, and the fact that it looks like it is still going on. Each time you hear of a horrific murder, you are looking to the one source that is supposed to be in the position to provide you with justice, and it is not there."*

She concluded by saying: *"I would support your call for a public inquiry that would get to the bottom of your brother's murder and the issues that led to his death. I can see why you are having an uphill struggle with this. This is a whole can of worms that you are opening...it is going to be a long struggle, and a lot of people will be covering their backs."*

Alastair's response was as equally telling: *"I am convinced that the Met's failure to deal with corruption when Daniel was murdered had a direct link with the poisoning of the inquiries into Stephen's murder and the corruption crisis as a whole. I also believe that the secret 'inquiry' [into police corruption] that they undertook while the Stephen Lawrence inquiry was taking place was designed purely to keep this scandal out of the public eye while they dealt with the outrage generated by Stephen's case. I think this is profoundly unhealthy, and we are determined not to let the government or the police get away with this."*

When the UK government announced the formation of the National Crime Agency, along similar lines to America's FBI, one of its first tasks was to lead an investigation into claims that the killers of Stephen Lawrence had been shielded from prosecution by corrupt officers on behalf of Clifford Norris. Following allegations made against him during Mark Ellison's judicial review of the case, a particular point of reference was the conduct of John Davidson during the original investigation.

On hearing the news of the latest investigation into the circumstances surrounding her son's senseless murder, Doreen Lawrence said: *"We ask those that have any information, be they former police officers or criminals, to examine their conscience. They should come forward, so justice can be done. Police corruption has denied us, and others, justice. It is a denial of the trust the police and state have placed in them by citizens. Those who betray the trust placed in them, should face justice, whenever it catches up with them."*

Mrs Lawrence was awarded the OBE in 2003 for services to community relations and 10 years later became a life peer. Baroness Lawrence of Clarendon was named the UK's most important woman by BBC Radio 4's *Woman's Hour* in 2014. Home Secretary Theresa May said of her: *"'What is most striking about this woman is the great strength that she has shown over decades - strength to carry on, to keep on going, even in the most difficult times when all seemed impossible."*

3

The Inquest, the Evidence and Friends in Fleet Street

When Alex Marunchak of the *News of the World* did finally break his silence on the Daniel Morgan murder case, it was to conduct an interview with his friend and close business associate, Jonathan Rees. The article, Marunchak's only one on the subject, was published on the 14th May 1989, shortly after charges against Rees had been dropped by the Crown Prosecution Service, and more than two years after Morgan's slaying. During the course of the interview, Rees maintained that Morgan had been murdered by a team of corrupt police officers who were concerned about the potential publication of the story that Morgan and Holmes were trying to sell. In hindsight, his claims may have some credibility. However, there is no doubt whatsoever that Rees, rather disparagingly described on the front page of *The Sun* in April 1988 as *"pint-size John Rees"*, would have known the officers involved and deliberately withheld that information from the investigation.

Indeed, Duncan Hanrahan, in his testimony to the 1988 inquest into Daniel Morgan's death, claimed, amongst other things, that Rees had told him that he had information that could lead to Morgan's killers but that he would not divulge it because of what he saw as his shoddy treatment at the hands of Detective Chief Superintendent Douglas Campbell and his team.

A further claim that was made at the inquest, and again substantiated by book keeper Kevin Lennon, was that the location for the murder was not at all random and that the Golden Lion had been carefully chosen by the perpetrators in the knowledge that the crime would be investigated by detectives from Catford police station, and would include among their number Detective Sergeant Sid Fillery.

Although Scotland Yard had advised the Morgan family that it would not be necessary for them to be legally represented at the inquest, their suspicions were aroused, and with some assistance they were able to retain the services of barrister June Tweedie. Tweedie had lately been involved in the inquest into the controversial killing of three IRA suspects in Gibraltar at the hands of the SAS.

Marunchak's interview with Jonathan Rees in the *New of the World*

She put it to Lennon that *"the reason for the murder being carried out in that area was because those same Catford police officers* [the officers with whom Lennon claimed Rees had told him he had been conspiring] *would then be involved in the murder investigation and would suppress any information linking the murder to Jon Rees or themselves?"*

Lennon simply replied, *"That is right."*

The inquest also heard from Margaret Harrison, the estate agent with whom Daniel Morgan had a rendezvous shortly before his death. It was put to her that she had received over sixty phone calls from Morgan's business partner, Jonathan Rees, in the months leading up to March 1987. Asked to explain these calls, she categorically denied having an affair with Rees behind Morgan's back, and told the inquest that this could not have been a source of antipathy between the two men, nor could it have been a motive for Daniel's murder. Shortly after the inquest, Harrison and Rees moved into a house together in South London.

Although the inquest jury returned a verdict of unlawful killing, Alastair Morgan and his family were incensed when the police took no further action. Detective Chief Superintendent Campbell had already admitted that flaws in the initial investigation had made it almost impossible to bring a successful prosecution.

Even before the inquest had started, and following Sid Fillery's departure from the Met, Alastair had begun to lobby politicians over concerns of police complicity. According to Gillard and Flynn in *"The Untouchables"*, Alastair had written to the then home secretary Douglas Hurd. He stated: *"I stressed strongly in my letter that the inference of possible police involvement in the murder was now very serious"*. The home secretary was not inclined to act. In a letter to the late Paul Keel, then of the *Guardian*, Alastair expressed his concerns about police corruption in relation to the case by saying: *"The really good ones* [police officers] *get harassed out by cynical and complacent colleagues."*

Because of the nature of the case and the strong suggestion of police corruption, Alastair assumed that the media, particularly the tabloids, would be queueing up with him to expose the truth. *"I had this idea in my head of the press fearlessly probing into areas where people did not want them to look."* However, they didn't, and the general lack of interest in Fleet Street initially baffled him. As the years rolled by and more and more details emerged regarding the relationships between the press, officers of the Met and Southern Investigations, Morgan's confusion began to clear. It was replaced by a feeling of betrayal.

He and his family began a lengthy campaign for

justice. A campaign that is still active today. It was a campaign that would eventually expose a nexus of corrupt police officers, dangerous criminals and tabloid journalists. It would shake the highest echelons of Scotland Yard and Fleet Street to their foundations. The mighty and the once untouchable would find themselves falling from grace one after another. Some lost their jobs, some, like bent cop Duncan Hanrahan and former Conservative Party communications director Andy Coulson, would find themselves behind bars.

The world's one time best-selling newspaper was closed down amid revelations of institutionalised malpractice by members of its staff. *The News of the World* signed off in July 2011 by declaring: *"Phones were hacked, and for that this newspaper is truly sorry...there is no justification for this appalling wrongdoing."* It was replaced as *The Sun's* sister paper little more than six months later by *The Sun on Sunday* who retained many former *News of the World* employees. Various internet domain names containing the phrase "sunonsunday" had been registered by News International on July 5th 2011, 5 days prior to the *News of the World's* tearful demise.

Rupert Murdoch, the billionaire media mogul and chairman of the *News of the World's* parent company, News Corporation, was flown into London to stand before a parliamentary select committee of MPs. His son, James Murdoch, was also called to give evidence. Murdoch was described by the committee, as *"not fit"* to be in charge of a major company. James was criticised for showing *"wilful ignorance"* in connection to phone hacking at the newspaper.

The *News of the World* had first been published as long ago as 1843 and was aimed squarely at the newly literate working classes, featuring stories about vice, prostitution, and crime. Legendary newspaperman and editor of the Pall Mall Gazette between its founding in 1865 and his resignation from the post in 1880, Frederick Greenwood, once famously said of the fledgling *News of the World*, *"I looked at it and then I put it in the waste-paper basket. And then I thought, 'If I leave it there the cook may read it' so I burned it."* Despite its detractors, the *News of the World* grew from strength to strength and by the 1950s had become the world's biggest selling newspaper, sometimes selling over 9 million copies.

Rupert and James Murdoch appearing before the House of Commons Select Committee to give evidence relating to phone hacking (Photo: PA)

In 2011, it was described as *"the greatest newspaper in the world"* by its then editor, Colin Myler. It won four awards at that year's prestigious British Press Awards including News Reporter of the Year which, ironically, went to Mazher Mahmood for his story about Pakistani cricketers and the spot-fixing scandal. Perhaps even more ironic was that the award for Newspaper of the Year was won by *The Guardian* who had led the investigation into the phone hacking scandal that was to shortly end a 168-year-old publishing institution.

The *News of the World* had survived two world wars and dozens of libel actions but it could not survive the exposure of the nefarious techniques its reporters and senior staff employed to gather information in pursuit of its stories.

The phone hacking scandal was uncovered much by accident during ongoing investigations into corruption within the Metropolitan Police Service; investigations that were, in some part, initiated by Alastair Morgan's unwillingness to be silenced over his brother's murder more than two decades earlier.

There were to be survivors of these investigations though. Former detectives Fillery, Davidson, Coles, and Adams all survived (if you put to one side Fillery's indecency conviction) and were all rewarded with full police pensions. Charges against Alex Marunchak were dropped by the CPS in September 2015. Coincidentally, it was also in September 2015 that Rebekah Brooks was re-instated as Chief Executive of Rupert Murdoch's rebranded News UK. She has become one of the phone hacking scandal's greatest survivors. Brooks had been the editor of The *News of the World* from 2000 until she left to become editor of its sister paper, *The Sun,* in 2003.

During her tenure as *News of the World* editor, and whilst Andy Coulson was her deputy, she oversaw the coverage of the investigations into the abductions and murders of two young girls. Sarah Payne was first reported missing on 1st July 2000 and Milly Dowler on 21st March 2002. The investigations into both disappearances and the aftermath of the girls' murders would become indelibly linked with the career of Rebekah Brooks.

On the 17th July 2000, the naked remains of 8 year-old Sarah Payne were discovered in a field in West Sussex. Roy Whiting was arrested on 6th February 2001 and charged with murder. He was sentenced to life imprisonment in January the following year. A known paedophile, Whiting had already been questioned and later released by the police on two separate occasions prior to being charged. The first of these was on 2nd July 2000, the day after Sarah's disappearance when she may still have been alive. During the course of his trial, it emerged that Whiting had a previous conviction dating back to 1995 when he was sentenced to four years for attacking another 8 year-old girl, and was already on the Sex Offenders Register.

Sarah's parents were clearly distraught, and the fact that Roy Whiting's background had been known only to the police made their pain even harder to bear. They began a campaign for what they called "Sarah's Law", which demanded public access to the Sex Offenders Register. Their campaign received the very public support of the mighty *News of the World* under the stewardship of Rebekah Brooks. It seems that staff at the newspaper neglected to inform Sarah's mother that they had been hacking her voicemails. The *News of the World* demanded that those suspected of being convicted child sex offenders should be *"named and shamed"*. Their campaign led to suspected offenders being attacked in public, many of them in cases of mistaken identity. Child protection groups were concerned that such vigilantism would drive paedophiles "underground", thereby making it more difficult for the police to monitor their activities. The Chief Constable of Gloucestershire described the newspaper's campaign as *"grossly irresponsible"*. Meanwhile, Brooks appeared on the BBC with David Frost to defend her campaign by saying, it was *"only right that the public have access"* to the identities of sex offenders. One such instance of public conscience involved a respected paediatrician who had her house vandalised by an angry mob who thought that her occupation meant that she was a paedophile.

Schoolgirl Milly Dowler was just 13-years-old when, in March 2002, she was snatched on her way home from school in Walton-on-Thames, Surrey. It wasn't until September and following an extensive police search that her body was finally discovered hidden in woods in Hampshire. In the summer of 2011 a serial killer called Levi Bellfield who was already serving three life sentences for the murder of two young women and the attempted murder of a third was convicted of Milly Dowler's abduction and murder and given an additional life sentence. Whilst in prison, he later confessed to the crime, claiming that he had raped and tortured his victim for fourteen hours before he then strangled her and dumped her body.

Following Bellfield's trial, it was revealed that even in the first days of the 2002 police investigation into Milly Dowler's disappearance, her phone had been hacked by the *News of the World* whose editor at the time was Rebekah Brooks. Personal messages left by her distraught parents pleading with the teenager to get in touch with them were covertly listened to by journalists from the paper. Some of these messages were later deleted in order to make room for more messages that could then be used as background for their news reports. At the time, the Dowler family believed, with apparent justification, that Milly was deleting her own voicemails and were therefore convinced that she was still alive.

In an article first published in *The Guardian* on Monday 4th July 2011, investigative journalist Nick Davies and colleague Amelia Hill reported as follows:

"The Guardian investigation has shown that, within a very short time of Milly vanishing, News of the World journalists reacted by engaging in what was standard practice in their newsroom: they hired private investigators to get them a story."

"Their first step was simple, albeit illegal. Paperwork seen by the Guardian reveals that they paid a Hampshire private investigator, Steve Whittamore, to obtain home addresses and, where necessary, ex-directory phone numbers for any families called Dowler in the Walton area. The three addresses Whittamore found could be obtained lawfully on the electoral register. The two ex-directory numbers, however, were 'blagged' illegally from British Telecom's confidential records by one of Whittamore's associates, John Gunning, who works from a base in Wiltshire. One of the ex-directory

numbers was attributed by Whittamore to Milly's family home."

"Then, with the help of its own full-time private investigator, Glenn Mulcaire, the News of the World started illegally intercepting mobile phone messages. Scotland Yard is now investigating evidence that the paper hacked directly into the voicemail of the missing girl's own phone. As her friends and parents called and left messages imploring Milly to get in touch with them, the News of the World was listening and recording their every private word."

"But the journalists at the News of the World then encountered a problem. Milly's voicemail box filled up and would accept no more messages. Apparently thirsty for more information from more voicemails, the paper intervened – and deleted the messages that had been left in the first few days after her disappearance. According to one source, this had a devastating effect: when her friends and family called again and discovered that her voicemail had been cleared, they concluded that this must have been done by Milly herself and, therefore, that she must still be alive. But she was not. The interference created false hope and extra agony for those who were misled by it."

"The Dowler family then granted an exclusive interview to the News of the World in which they talked about their hope, quite unaware that it had been falsely kindled by the newspaper's own intervention. Sally Dowler told the paper: 'If Milly walked through the door, I don't think we'd be able to speak. We'd just weep tears of joy and give her a great big hug.'"

Davies and Hill's article remains an excellent insight into how the *News of the World* and its fellow Fleet Street tabloids operated prior to the Leveson Inquiry. It should be pointed out though that subsequent to the publication of their article, the Metropolitan Police later concluded that although the *News of the World* did indeed hack Milly's voicemails, it was "*unlikely to have been responsible for the deletion of a set of voicemails from the phone that caused her parents to have false hopes that she was alive."*

The hacking of Milly Dowler's phone had further implications with regard to the police investigation into her disappearance. The same article goes on to explain:

"The deletion of the messages also caused difficulties for the police by confusing the picture when they had few leads to pursue. It also potentially destroyed valuable evidence."

"According to one senior source familiar with the Surrey police investigation: 'It can happen with abduction murders that the perpetrator will leave messages, asking the missing person to get in touch, as part of their efforts at concealment. We need those messages as evidence. Anybody who destroys that evidence is seriously interfering with the course of a police investigation.'"

"The paper made little effort to conceal the hacking from its readers. On 14 April 2002 it published a story about a woman allegedly pretending to be Milly Dowler who had applied for a job with a recruitment agency: 'It is thought the hoaxer even gave the agency Milly's real mobile number ... the agency used the number to contact Milly when a job vacancy arose and left a message on her voicemail ... it was on March 27, six days after Milly went missing, that the employment agency appears to have phoned her mobile.'"

"The newspaper also made no effort to conceal its activity from Surrey police. After it had hacked the message from the recruitment agency on Milly's phone, the paper informed police about it."

"It was Surrey detectives who established that the call was not intended for Milly Dowler. At the time, Surrey police suspected that phones belonging to detectives and to Milly's parents also were being targeted."

"One of those [police officers] who was involved in the original inquiry said: 'We'd arrange landline calls.

We didn't trust our mobiles.'"

It is clear from statements made by officers at the time of the investigation into Milly Dowler's disappearance that the police were aware that journalist (or their agents) from the *News of the World* were employing illegal methods to gather information on the case. If this was so, why were these breaches not investigated? According to Davies and Hill, *"...they* [the police] *took no action against the News of the World, partly because their main focus was to find the missing schoolgirl and partly because this was only one example of tabloid misbehaviour. As one source close to the inquiry put it: 'There was a hell of a lot of dirty stuff going on.'"*

In another article published by *The Guardian*, this time in April 2013, Vikram Dodd asks that very question. So too had the Independent Police Complaints Commission (IPCC) during their 2011 investigation. Dodd wrote: *"The revelation of the hacking of the murdered teenager's phone by the News of the World led to revulsion that triggered the tabloid's closure. The IPCC found that there was knowledge of the alleged hacking 'at all levels' of the Surrey police team investigating the case, and that its head, Craig Denholm, even received documents mentioning it. But nothing was done for almost a decade, even after the 2007 conviction of a journalist from the paper for hacking the royal family and a private investigator for carrying it out."*

The private investigator referred to was Glenn Mulcaire. He, along with *News of the World* royal editor Clive Goodman, had been imprisoned in 2007 for illegally intercepting phone messages from Clarence House. A full-time investigator for the paper on a salary of approximately £100,000 a year, Mulcaire later admitted to hacking Milly Dowler's phone on behalf of the *News of the World.* It was through documents recovered during their investigation into Mulcaire that led police to believe that there were as many as 4,744 potential victims of the *News of the World* phone hacking scandal.

"But," Dodd continues, *"the IPCC said they could not find evidence to disprove the assertion by Denholm, now deputy chief constable of Surrey, that he did not know and did not make the 'relevant connections'".*

"Thus he will not face any disciplinary charge but Surrey announced he will receive words of advice, the lowest form of sanction. He is eligible to retire soon, by 2014, on a pension estimated at over £80,000 a year."

In conclusion of their investigation, the IPCC released a damning statement: *"There is no doubt, from our investigation and the evidence gathered by Operation Baronet, that Surrey police knew in 2002 of the allegation that Milly Dowler's phone had been hacked by the News of the World. It is apparent from the evidence that there was knowledge of this at all levels within the investigation team. There is equally no doubt that Surrey police did nothing to investigate; nobody was arrested or charged in relation to the alleged interception either in 2002 or subsequently, until the Operation Weeting arrests in 2011. Phone hacking was a crime in 2002 and it should have been investigated. Our investigation has heard from officers and former officers at Surrey police who have expressed surprise and dismay that this was not done. We have not been able to uncover any evidence, in documentation or witness statements, of why and by whom that decision was made: former senior officers in particular appear to be afflicted by a form of COLLECTIVE AMNESIA about this. This is perhaps not surprising, given the events of 2011 and the public outcry that the hacking of Milly Dowler phone produced."*

They also referenced claims by serving Surrey police officers of the time that the force had an *"unhealthy relationship"* with the media. The IPCC concluded that this was to *"keep the media onside."*

When Sir John Stevens had become commissioner of the Met in 2000, he immediately set out to improve their tarnished public image by initiating closer ties with the media. In early 2000, Dick Fedorcio, the Met's Director of Public Affairs, convened a meeting between Commissioner Stevens and none other than Rebekah Brooks and Alex Marunchak. It was at this point that the *News of the World* was able to strengthen its connections with the Metropolitan Police Service at the very highest levels. The question is: Who was keeping who "onside"?

When Stevens retired as Metropolitan Police Commissioner in 2005, he landed a lucrative contract as a columnist for the *News of the World*. He was later investigated by the Independent Police Complaints Commission for his role in Scotland Yard's handling of the Stephen Lawrence case. Press officer Fedorcio resigned his post in 2012 following an unconnected IPCC investigation into his conduct. With regard to Fedorcio's case, Deborah Glass of the IPCC announced that, in 2011, they had decided to investigate *"the relationship between Mr Fedorcio and Neil Wallis, a former deputy editor at the News of the World... Our investigation found that Mr Fedorcio has a case to answer.... Last week the Metropolitan Police Service proposed to initiate proceedings for gross misconduct and I agreed with that proposal."*

Following *The Guardian's* revelations regarding the conduct of the *News of the Word's* reporters during the investigation into Milly Dowler's disappearance and her subsequent murder nine years previously, the Dowler's family lawyer Mark Lewis made a statement on their behalf in which he said: *"It is distress heaped upon tragedy to learn that the News of the World had no humanity at such a terrible time. The fact that they were prepared to act in such a heinous way that could have jeopardised the police investigation and give them false hope is despicable."*

New York Times reporter Sarah Lyall wrote that should the allegations against the *News of the World* prove to be with foundation, *"it would mean either that Ms. Brooks had no idea how the paper she edited was obtaining information about the Dowler family for its articles, or that she knew about the hacking and allowed it."* Either way, July 2011 was not a good month for Ms Brooks.

The influence of the Milly Dowler phone-hacking scandal on the closure of the *News of the World* cannot be overstated. When allegations were then made that they had also hacked into the private messages of the bereaved families of service personnel killed in action, it was the final straw. The public were outraged and advertising was withdrawn. The paper ceased publication on July 10th. When Rebekah Brooks, who was by now Chief Executive Officer of News Corp, the UK arm of News International, made the announcement there were obvious rumblings of discontent among the newspaper's staff, some of whom claimed that their jobs had all been sacrificed to save hers.

Questions were asked in parliament. Leader of the opposition Ed Milliband said that Brooks should *"consider her position"*. Prime Minister David Cameron who was a friend of hers commented that if Brooks had offered her resignation to him, he would have accepted it. Milly Dowler's disgusted parents also demanded that Brooks should go.

On July 15th she did go. She went with a £10.8 million pay off from News Corp as *"compensation for loss of office"* and was told by her boss, Rupert Murdoch, to travel the world on him for a year. But two days later she was arrested. Her former colleagues, Andy Coulson and Neil Wallis had already been arrested only days earlier. All three of them were charged with offences relating to the phone-hacking scandal being investigated by officers of Operation Weeting. Brooks was also charged with conspiring to pervert the course of justice by frustrating the Met's investigation into the *News of the World*. During her trial, it emerged that she had once engaged in a six year affair with her former deputy editor Coulson. Coulson was found guilty of conspiring to intercept voicemails at the Old Bailey in June 2014 and was later sentenced to 18 months in prison. Some cynics believe that Coulson was sacrificed to save Brooks who was acquitted of all charges.

Rebekah Brooks and Rupert Murdoch

In September 2015, Rebekah Brooks returned to the rebranded News UK where she recommenced her previous role as its Chief Executive. Many viewed such an appointment with some scepticism. Shadow Culture Secretary, Chris Bryant, described it as ludicrous, and went on to say: *"Rupert Murdoch has just stuck two fingers up to the British public and the thousands of people whose phones were hacked by News International. However you cut it, his newspapers hacked thousands of phones and made money out of the private lives of ordinary members of the public who only came into the limelight because they were victims of crime. Hundreds of ordinary journalists lost their jobs when Mr Murdoch closed the News of the World, but it seems Rebekah Brooks is to get very special treatment. Clearly Mr Murdoch was only feigning humility when he appeared before the DCMS* [Department of Culture, Media and Sport] S*elect Committee."*

But illegal activities such as phone hacking had been going on at the *News of the World* long before

Brooks and Coulson's tenures as editor. Alex Marunchak and other *News of the World* journalists had held close relationships with Southern Investigations and their network of corrupt police officers since at least 1988. The services of Jonathan Rees, Sid Fillery and their dubious associates had been regularly employed by the newspaper's staff for many years prior to the abduction of Milly Dowler.

In 1994, Piers Morgan was editor of the paper. During his editorship, he admits that the *News of the World* had spies at two of their Fleet Street rivals. They paid staff at the *Sunday Mirror* and the *Sunday People* to keep them updated on forthcoming stories. Morgan said of this in his own book, *The Insider,* "*It's a disgrace, of course, and totally unethical.*" When he became editor of the *Daily Mirror* the following year, he had the "spies" sacked.

Piers Morgan was questioned on two separate occasions, in 2013 and 2015, by detectives investigating the phone-hacking scandal. He has always denied any knowledge of such practices, stating on CNN in the United States in July 2011: "*For the record, in my time at the News of the World and the Mirror, I have never hacked a phone, told anyone to hack a phone, or published any stories based on the hacking of a phone.*"

However these denials appear to be slightly at variance with an interview he gave to the Press Gazette in 2007 following the conviction of *News of the World* royal reporter Clive Goodman and shortly before the phone-hacking scandal got into full swing. In it, he said: "*As for Clive Goodman, I feel a lot of sympathy for a man who has been the convenient fall guy for an investigative practice that everyone knows was going on at almost every paper in Fleet Street for years.*" Morgan was called to appear before the Leveson Inquiry in December 2011 to explain these comments.

He appeared at the inquiry via a video-link from the United States. He is seen on screen sitting, not with the usual air of self-importance, but rather exhibiting the mannerisms of a nervous schoolboy being admonished by a disapproving master. Figures of national importance along with global superstars had felt duty-bound to appear in person to assist Lord Leveson with his inquiry into invasive media practises. Morgan, apparently, had not.

Former editor of both the *News of the World* and the *Daily* Mirror, Piers Morgan, gives evidence to the Leveson Inquiry

He gave evidence for nearly two hours, during the course of which, he was asked about the practice of recovering personal documents such as bank statements from dustbins belonging to celebrities. Morgan told Robert Jay QC that if someone throws something away, then it is not unethical to use it. *"If you throw rubbish into the street, I wonder how unethical it is if that then appears in a newspaper; it's rubbish, isn't it?"*

Jay later referred to Morgan's 2009 appearance on the BBC Radio 4 programme *Desert Island Discs* during which presenter Kirsty Young had asked him: *"And what about this nice middle-class boy who would have to be dealing with, I mean, essentially people who rake through people's bins for a living? People who tap people's phones, people who take secret photographs, who do all that very nasty down-in-the-gutter stuff. How did you feel about that?"*

Morgan's reply was startlingly revealing: *"To be honest, let's put that in perspective as well. Not a lot of that went on. A lot of it was done by third parties rather than the staff themselves. That's not to defend it, because obviously you were running the results of their work. I'm quite happy to be parked in the corner of tabloid beast and to have to sit here defending all these things I used to get up to, and I make no pretence about the stuff we used to do. I simply say the net of people doing it was very wide, and certainly encompassed the high and low end of the supposed newspaper market."* When Morgan talks of *"third parties"* is he referring to private investigators such as Steve Whittamore, Glenn Mulcaire, and Jonathan Rees?

Morgan told the Leveson Inquiry that he had misunderstood Ms Young's question and had not been referring to phone-hacking. *"No. In fact if you listen to the tape it's quite interesting. I go to answer her question straight away and she cuts me off... I was responding in general terms ... I wasn't alluding to phone tapping."* When pressed further by Robert Jay, he claimed: *"I've already tried to answer on the first point. I didn't hear her say 'phone tapping'. If you listen to it in real time I think you would see that."*

During his appearance on *Desert Island Discs,* Morgan also neglected to inform Ms Young that she too had been the victim of *"that very nasty down-in-the-gutter stuff".*

Another story from Morgan's book involved the actress Kate Winslett. He says that he arrived back at his office in April 2011 to find that Ms Winslett had left a message to say that she was pulling out of making an appearance at the *Daily Mirror* sponsored *Pride of Britain* awards. Finding that he had her number, Morgan elected to call her in an attempt to persuade her to change her mind. He doesn't elaborate on how he came to have the actress's personal phone number but glibly states, *"Someone had got hold of her mobile phone number – I never like to ask how – so I rang her."* The inference being that the number had been passed to someone at the *Daily Mirror* by a private investigator.

Ms Winslett was horrified that the tabloid had managed to procure her private phone number and, according to Morgan, asked him: *"How did you get my number, I've only just changed it. You've got to tell me, please. I am so worried now; if the press get my number, then I have to change it."*

Morgan says that he assured her: *"Relax Kate, I won't be giving it to anyone."*

In *The Insider*, he also boasted of resisting a legal challenge from Princess Diana's former lover, James Hewitt. Jamie Doward reports in an article published in *The Guardian* on 6th August 2011 that: *"Morgan wrote that Hewitt claimed he had not been paid for his collaboration on a book. Morgan replied: 'Yes you did – I saw your bank statements'. It is doubtful whether such information could have been obtained by anything other than illegal means. Hewitt is now in the process of reporting Morgan to the police, urging them to reopen an investigation into allegations surrounding the theft of his personal letters from the princess."*

Robert Jay asked Morgan about a further passage from the same book that also referred to Hewitt. Morgan had written: *"We were offered a dodgy transcript of a phone conversation between James Hewitt and Anna Ferretti today. My attention was drawn to a moment when she asks, 'If you don't win the case, will you kill Piers Morgan?'"*

"Hewitt replies, 'Maybe, I don't know, I don't know.' In another call, he expands on his thoughts, saying he knows a 'Nicaraguan hitman' who can take me out for £20,000!"

Robert Jay QC asked him why he had referred to the transcript as being *"dodgy"*.

Morgan replied that engaging the services of a hitman was *"dodgy"*.

Jay suggested to him that he may have been referring to the manner in which the transcript was obtained. Morgan dismissed such a suggestion.

In a 2006 column for the *Daily Mail*, Morgan had admitted that he had listened to a voicemail message that had been left by Sir Paul McCartney for his then wife Heather Mills. Sir Paul is described as sounding *"lonely, miserable and desperate"*.

Jamie Doward reports that *"The disclosure has prompted Mills to claim the message could have been heard only by hacking into her phone."*

When asked about this by Robert Jay, Morgan was not so forthcoming:

Jay: *"Have you listened to what you believe to be illegally obtained voice messages?"*

Morgan: *"I do not believe so, no."*

Jay asked him about the Paul McCartney message that he had previously claimed to have listened to.

Morgan replied: *"I can't discuss where I heard that tape or who made it."*

Jay asked him if it was a recording of a voice message.

Morgan: *"I listened to a tape of a message yes, I believe it was yes. I'm not going to discuss where I heard it or who played it to me."*

He was then asked if he thought that listening to someone else's personal messages without their consent, even if it is a tape recording, was unethical.

Morgan replied: *"It doesn't necessarily follow that listening to someone else talking to someone else is unethical."*

Lord Justice Leveson, however, disagreed with him.

When Morgan was asked about a digitally altered photograph of Princess Diana and Dodi Fayed that had been published by his newspaper in August 1997, he admitted *"it was a stupid thing to do."* The photograph had been doctored in order to make it look as though the couple were kissing. In his defence, Morgan said: *"We didn't actually con the public because it was exactly the same as the picture that was going to appear in a rival paper the next day."*

In his summing up of the evidence that Morgan

had given to the inquiry, Lord Leveson stated that his testimony relating to phone-hacking was *"utterly unpersuasive"* and that Morgan had been *"...aware that it was taking place in the press as a whole and that he was sufficiently unembarrassed by what was criminal behaviour that he was prepared to joke about it."*

Piers Morgan was sacked as editor of the Daily Mirror on 14th May 2004 following the publication by that newspaper of fake photographs purporting to show British soldiers of the Queen's Lancashire Regiment abusing an Iraqi prisoner. A former regiment commander said that the pictures had put the lives of troops in danger and had also acted as a recruiting poster for al-Qaeda.

Following the scandal, the *Daily Mirror* issued a statement in which it said that they had *"... published in good faith photographs which it absolutely believed were genuine images of British soldiers abusing an Iraqi prisoner. However there is now sufficient evidence to suggest that these pictures are fakes and that the Daily Mirror has been the subject of a calculated and malicious hoax. The Daily Mirror therefore apologises unreservedly for publishing the pictures and deeply regrets the reputational damage done to the QLR and the Army in Iraq. The paper will continue to cooperate fully with the investigation."*

"The board of Trinity Mirror has decided that it would be inappropriate for Piers Morgan to continue in his role as editor of the Daily Mirror and he will therefore be stepping down with immediate effect."

The BBC's Nicholas Witchell reported that: *"...it appeared Piers Morgan remained unrepentant right to the end. According to one report Mr Morgan refused the demand to apologise, was sacked and immediately escorted from the building."*

In February 2014, Morgan was also sacked by US television channel CNN when they ceased production of his chat show, *Piers Morgan Live.* This followed a 100,000 signature petition being delivered to the

White House demanding his deportation back to the UK. The news of his dismissal was received with delight by former adversaries such as fellow TV presenter Jeremy Clarkson (*"I understand that Nigerian TV is looking for a new chat show host. Anyone got any suggestions?"*), and former footballer, now the BBC's *Match of the Day* presenter, Gary Lineker (*"Who'd have thought he'd be ousted before* [Arsene] *Wenger?"*). Lineker's comment being a reference to Morgan's loudly and frequently voiced opinion that Arsenal football manager, Mr Wenger, ought to step down.

In April 2015, Piers Morgan was interviewed under caution by officers from the Met's Operation Golding as part of their ongoing investigation into allegations of phone-hacking at Mirror Group Newspapers during his tenure as editor of the *Daily Mirror*.

4

Kim James, Conspiracy and the Second and Third Investigations

In 1988, largely due to Alastair Morgan's perseverance, the Met voluntarily referred the investigation into his brother's death to the Police Complaints Authority who, in turn, appointed an outside force to look into complaints regarding the handling of the case.

In July that year a team of detectives from the Hampshire Constabulary began a review of the evidence. This new investigation was known as Operation Drake and its terms of reference were to *"investigate allegations that police were involved in the murder of Daniel Morgan and any other matters arising."* A secondary investigation was also launched, this time into the alibis of Jonathan Rees, Paul Goodridge, and Goodridge's girlfriend Jean Wisden who was suspected of conspiring to pervert the course of justice by providing false alibis.

Hampshire Police concluded their investigation in January 1989 with the announcement that they had found *"no evidence whatsoever"* to support allegations of criminal misconduct by officers of the Met. However, Jonathan Rees was again arrested, this time along with Goodridge, and both men were later charged with the murder.

Four months later, the Director of Public Prosecutions discontinued proceedings due to a lack of sufficient evidence and the charges against the pair were dropped.

Once more appalled by the Crown Prosecution Service's inability to mount a prosecution, let alone to secure a conviction, Alastair Morgan and his family stepped up their campaign for justice. They began to lobby their Members of Parliament along with senior Scotland Yard officers. In November 1997, this culminated in a meeting with the then Metropolitan Police Commissioner Sir Paul Condon who indicated his willingness to once more review the case.

At the time, Sir Paul was also under intense pressure over the Met's handling of the Stephen Lawrence case. Although he was to accept that mistakes had been made and was to later offer his apologies to Stephen's parents, he had refused to agree with Sir William McPherson that the Met's failings were, to some extent, a product of *"institutional racism"*.

Ten years after the second investigation into Daniel Morgan's murder, a third investigation was launched in 1998. Codenamed Operation Nigeria, and later changed to Operation Two Bridges, it was to be part of the ongoing investigation into police corruption being carried out by the Yard's notorious "ghost squad". It was headed by Deputy Assistant Commissioner Roy Clark and was so covert that even the Morgan family were unaware of its existence.

The investigation was two-fold. Firstly, it was intended to gather further evidence regarding the murder of Daniel Morgan and, secondly, to investigate allegations of police corruption, particularly in relation to Southern Investigations. It was suspected that Jonathan Rees was paying serving and former police officers for sensitive information and then selling it on to the highest bidder. In the event, Clark's investigation revealed far more than this and in years to come would have far reaching consequences.

With the personal authorization of Sir Paul Condon, the appropriate warrants were obtained and, in April 1999, Rees's offices in Grange Road, Thornton Heath were bugged. According to journalist Graeme McLagan of *The Guardian*, the officers carrying out the surveillance were given very specific instructions. They *"were warned not to leave the tiniest sign that anyone had been inside the premises, let alone planted a bug. 'They are alert, cunning and devious individuals who have current knowledge of investigative methods and techniques which may be used against them,' said an internal report. 'Such is their level of access to individuals within the police, through professional and social contacts, that the threat of compromise to any conventional investigation against them is constant and very real.'"*

The surveillance operation began to pay dividends almost immediately. Rees was overheard telling somebody that he was waiting for a police contact to provide him with information about "*the desecration of the street memorial*" to Stephen Lawrence. The implication being that a client had asked Rees to find out what the police knew about the perpetrators of the repeated vandalism. The *Daily Mail* asked the following question: *"If so, who was asking the bent private detective for Lawrence-related police intelligence?"*

It is thought that, at the time, Rees was receiving in the region of £150,000 a year from the *News of the World* in return for illegally sourced information. In his own words: *"No one pays like the News of the World do."* He was also heard to threaten Alex Marunchak that his bosses at the paper could easily *"get f...ing tipped off about who gets f...ing backhanders."*

Some of the information he traded was sensitive police information. At one point, he was heard telling someone about a story he had sold to an, as yet, unnamed reporter. The story related to Kenny Noye of Brinks Mat fame and his recent extradition from Spain for the murder of Stephen Cameron. Rees openly admitted to providing the reporter with details about how the police finally tracked Noye down with the help of GCHQ. He also gave him exact details of how and when Noye would be transported between Belmarsh Prison and the Old Bailey courtroom where he was to stand trial; information that was, of course, of a highly sensitive nature.

In July 1999, a telephone conversation between Jonathan Rees and a Detective Constable Tom Kingston was recorded. Kingston was a serving officer with the South East Regional Crime Squad but at the time was suspended from duty and awaiting trial for his part in the theft of 2kg of amphetamine powder from a drugs dealer. Kingston was subsequently prosecuted and imprisoned.

During the call, Kingston was heard telling Rees about a royal couple who were having marriage difficulties. Kingston said that he had received the information from a fellow serving officer whose duties included protecting the royal family. According to the CIB transcript of the call, Rees wanted to know if the couple were *"still living together?"*

As that call ended, Rees immediately telephoned his friend Alex Marunchak at the *News of the World*. *"You know the information I gave you about Noye?"* he was heard to say to Marunchak, before going on to tell him that he had received a new story from the same source involving a minor royal couple and thus apparently confirming DC Kingston as his source for the Kenneth Noye story and Marunchak as the recipient. Kingston was also caught collecting sums of cash from Southern Investigations as payment for himself and for his contact in the diplomatic protection squad.

Graeme McLagan wrote: *"In July 1999 the bugging operation captured a conversation between Rees and another corrupt serving detective, Tom Kingston - later jailed for drug theft - in which they discussed a police contact in the diplomatic protection squad at Buckingham Palace whose firearms certificate was withdrawn because he had been taking steroids."*

"On July 28, the story appeared in the Mirror under reporter Gary Jones's byline with the headline 'Drug Claim Royal Cop in Gun Ban'. Mr Jones told us: 'We used the agency on occasion. They came on with the odd tip, what they'd heard from the Old Bill.'"

Conversations were recorded in which Rees and his associates discussed his old friend, Duncan Hanrahan. Hanrahan had retired from the Met in 1991 on medical grounds and had later established his own firm of private investigators with another former detective, Martin King. When Hanrahan and King were arrested for attempting to bribe a high ranking anti-corruption officer in 1997, Hanrahan became a CIB informant but was sentenced to 8 years and 4 months in March 1999, the month before the surveillance operation against Southern Investigations began.

Remarkably, although Hanrahan was in custody and was still, apparently, being debriefed by CIB, it seems that he was able to pass information onto Jonathan Rees who was recorded saying: *"Hanrahan said they keep talking about the Morgan murder every time they see me."*

When television presenter, Jill Dando, was shot dead outside her Fulham home on April 25th 1999, it became one of Britain's most high profile murder cases. Ms Dando was grabbed from behind, forced to the ground, and shot once through the head at point-blank range with a gun that had been fitted with a silencer. The killer, who left no evidence at the scene whatsoever apart from the single bullet that killed her, then made his escape in broad daylight in a busy London Street without anybody noticing. It was a classic contract-style hit. Criminologist David Wilson later confirmed: *"Everything about this murder screams out professional hit. It has all the hallmarks."*

It is surprising then that initial inquiries focussed on a local misfit called Barry George. Beside his extraordinarily odd behaviour, George had a history of committing sexual offences. Because of this he had previously been interviewed by police in connection with another high-profile murder case; that of the 1992 sexually motivated killing of Rachel Nickell on nearby Wimbledon Common. George's alibi for the Dando murder was that he had been stalking another woman at the time.

Ms Dando had not been sexually assaulted and experts agreed that a man such as Barry George, with a history of learning difficulties and a propensity to relate his every thought to complete strangers, was incapable of executing such a meticulously planned crime. Despite this he was convicted of murder on the flimsiest of evidence in July 2001 and sentenced to life imprisonment. The fragility of the conviction was later exposed in a retrial in 2008 in which Mr George had his conviction overturned.

In the immediate aftermath of Jill Dando's murder, various theories began to emerge. These included the supposition that Ms Dando had been the subject of an IRA or a Serbian hit squad. Another was that she had been targeted by a criminal gang because of her work for the *Crimewatch* television programme. The National Criminal Intelligence Service even managed to link Ms Dando's murder to Kenneth Noye. That particular theory being that an associate of Noye's called Joe travelled from Spain to London with the specific intention of killing the presenter in revenge for her *Crimewatch* appeal following the M25 road rage murder for which Noye was currently serving life in prison. It is said that Joe carried out the killing to improve his standing amongst the ex-pat criminal community in Spain and with Noye in particular. There is no evidence to suggest that Joe carried out this outrage with Mr Noye's knowledge, let alone consent. Nor, it seems, is there very much evidence to suggest that he carried it out at all.

In recent years though, an even more troubling motive has begun to emerge from the darkness. Friends, acquaintances, and colleagues of the former television presenter have come forward to claim that she was investigating a paedophile ring operating at the BBC involving established personalities such as Jimmy Savile and Stuart Hall and that she was preparing to reveal her findings to a *Panorama* documentary team.

Sir Jimmy Savile's sexual predilection for children was the worst kept secret at the BBC for many years. Archive footage of early episodes of *Top of the Pops* clearly shows him openly groping female members of his teenage audience. But it wasn't until after his death in 2011 that the full extent of his activities was publicly exposed by an ITV documentary crew.

However, as long ago as 1978, at the height of the punk rock phenomenon, a 22-year old Johnny Rotten, controversial singer with the Sex Pistols, gave a typically forthright interview to Vivienne Goldman of BBC Radio in which he said: *"I'd like to kill Jimmy Savile. I think he's a hypocrite. I bet he's into all kinds of seediness that we all know about but are not allowed to talk about. I know some rumours...I bet none of this'll be allowed out."*

Ms Goldman tells him: *"I should imagine libellous stuff won't be allowed out."*

The singer's response is emphatic: *"Nothing I've said is libel."*

But he was right; none of it was allowed out. The interview was canned and the Sex Pistols were subsequently banned from BBC Radio on the grounds of their outlandish behaviour.

When a mature John Lydon later appeared on *Piers Morgan's Life Stories* in September 2015, his host asked him about the 1978 BBC interview and Savile's subsequent exposure as a serial paedophile.

Lydon: *"We all knew what that cigar muncher was up to...but I'm very very bitter that the likes of Savile and the rest of them were allowed to continue."*

Morgan: *"Did you ever try and do anything about Savile?"*

Lydon: *"I did my bit. I said what I had to."*

Morgan: *"Did they air that? No. It just got supressed for legal reasons."*

Lydon: *"Yeah, and I found myself being banned from BBC Radio there for quite a while for my contentious behaviour."*

Morgan: *"But it's shocking. He got away with it for another thirty odd years."*

Lydon: *"Not only him but a whole bunch of them. And these are the purveyors of good taste...Well, I'm still here and the rest of them that are still alive...nice bit of jail time for them."*

No one knows how many of Savile's victims could have been spared their fate had more people taken Lydon's stance and publicly or otherwise aired their suspicions. It appears that Jill Dando was about to do just that when she was clinically executed by a professional contract killer.

At the time of Jill Dando's shooting, Jonathan Rees was heard by officers of CIB3's "ghost squad" boasting that he had a police source close to the investigation. Their transcripts read: *"There's big stories nearly every day with good information on the Jill Dando murder. We found out one of our bestest friends is also on that murder squad, but he ain't told us nothing. We only found out yesterday after that torrent of abuse we initially gave him. He's going to phone us today."*

Rees was also recorded obtaining classified information about the Chilean dictator General Pinochet who was, at the time, under house arrest in Surrey awaiting an extradition hearing. Another story that was being fed to Rees by his network of police contacts was that of London nail bomber, David Copeland, who was in Belmarsh awaiting trial. During one telephone conversation, Rees asks: *"...if he can find out more about Copeland and the messages he's receiving from God"*.

The anti-corruption unit's own report into the surveillance operation reveals: *"Rees and [others] are actively pursuing contacts with the police and business community to identify potential newsworthy stories. They then sell the information to the national media. The investigation has so far identified a serving police officer who has supplied confidential information and private investigators who can supply phone and bank accounts details of any person."*

On 11th March 2011, Nick Davies of *The Guardian* published an article in which he wrote: *"The bug betrayed the sheer speed and ease with which Rees was able to penetrate the flimsy fence of privacy that shields the vast reservoir of personal information now held on the databases controlled by the police and the DVLA, the phone companies and banks...When the Daily Mirror wanted the private mortgage details of all the governors of the Bank of England, Rees delivered...When the Sunday Mirror wanted to get inside the bank accounts of Prince Edward and the Countess of Wessex, it was equally easy..."*

Davies goes on to reproduce the partial transcript of a telephone conversation picked up by the surveillance team. Rees is discussing a story about the royal couple with a reporter, thought to be Gary Jones of the *Mirror.*

Reporter: *"Do you remember a couple of months ago, you got me some details on Edward's business and Sophie's business and how well they were doing?"*

Rees: *"Yeah"*

Reporter: *"And you did a check on Sophie's bank account."*

Rees: *"Yeah."*

Reporter: *"Is it possible to do that again? I'm not exactly sure what they're after but they seem to be under the impression that, you know, she was in the paper the other day for appearing in Hello! magazine. They think she's had some kind of payment off them."*

Rees: *"What? Off Hello!?"*

Reporter: *"Um, yeah."*

Rees: *"... find out how much."*

Reporter: *"Well, we just want to see if there's been any change to her bank account."*

Rees is later heard telling Jones to be careful *"because what we're doing is illegal, isn't it? I don't want people coming in and nicking us for a criminal offence, you know."* But he did get "nicked" for a criminal offense shortly afterwards.

Despite very little new evidence relating to the Daniel Morgan murder case being unearthed, by September 1999 Deputy Assistant Commissioner Clark's "ghost squad" were accumulating a mass of evidence involving various corrupt police officers and their contacts at Southern Investigations and in Fleet Street. They had documentary evidence of at least thirty crimes having been committed. As the Met began to build their case, it was hoped that they would be able to bring charges against at least one of the journalists who were in receipt of illicit information from Southern Investigations. An internal police report stated: *"The Metropolitan Police Service will undoubtedly benefit if a journalist is convicted of corrupting serving police officers. This will send a clear message to members of the media to consider their own ethical and illegal involvement with employees in the MPS in the future."*

The names of three Fleet Street employees had come to prominence during the course of the investigation. Those of Alex Marunchak of the *News of the World*, Doug Kempster of the *Sunday Mirror,* and a former colleague of Marunchak's, Gary Jones, who was now a reporter for Piers Morgan's *Daily Mirror.* However, no charges against any of the three were brought. The investigation, along with the surveillance operation, came to a premature close by events outside the control of Roy Clark and his team.

During the recording of conversations taking place at Rees's offices, it had become increasingly apparent that a serious crime was being planned and had it been allowed to run its course in the interest of more evidence gathering, a serious miscarriage of justice may well have been allowed to take place. Roy Clark had a difficult decision to make. Operation Two Bridges was halted.

Early in 2000 a report of the operation was submitted by the Met's head of anti-corruption, Commander Bob Quick, in which he detailed journalistic crimes, named specific journalists, and recommended further action be taken against those journalists. One of the reporters he named as deserving of further investigation was Alex Marunchak. Quick delivered his report in the weeks shortly before Sir John Stevens met with a delegation from News International in order to improve the Met's relationship with the media and to repair some of the damage that had been inflicted upon its reputation by the publicly perceived mishandling of the Stephen Lawrence investigation.

The party he met with included Rebekah Brooks, the recently appointed editor of the *News of the World,* and her colleague, Alex Marunchak. No further action against the journalists was taken and Quick's report was discarded.

Kim James was a 28 year-old former model who had once dated footballer Stan Collymore. Now working as a nursery nurse, she had recently endured acrimonious divorce proceedings following her marriage to a wealthy jeweller of allegedly dubious character called Simon James in 1995. Their divorce was finalised in April 1999 and shortly afterwards, the couple found themselves embroiled in a bitter custody battle over their two-year-old son. In his desperation to secure custody of his son, Simon James approached Jonathan Rees and his firm of private investigators, now called Law and Commercial, and asked them to obtain information against his ex-wife that would damage her case in forthcoming court proceedings. He painted her as a sexually promiscuous drug dealer who was unfit to care for the child.

In the event, and despite his numerous contacts, Rees was unable to obtain any information at all detrimental to Kim James's case. Indeed, officers of Operation Two Bridges were to overhear him tell James: *"One of our surveillance team is a police motorcyclist on the drugs squad, and he works for us on the side. It's a couple of years before he retires from the squad. He did a check on her, but there's nothing on the files. She doesn't come up associated with any drugs dealers."*

Not to be discouraged by this untimely set-back, and ignoring entirely the possibility that Ms James may well have been of exemplary character, the

77

resourceful Mr Rees devised an alternative plan. In exchange for £8,000 he would have a large quantity of cocaine planted in the target's car, the police would be tipped off, Kim James would be arrested and once convicted receive a substantial custodial sentence. Rees's plan would ensure Simon James custody of his son. Unfortunately the plan had one major flaw: the plotters were unaware that anti-corruption officers from CIB3 were listening to every word of it.

Rees assembled his team. A long-standing associate of his called Jimmy Cook would be hired to plant the drugs in Ms James's Fiat Punto. Mr Cook, incidentally, was later to be heavily implicated in the murder of Daniel Morgan. Unfortunately for Cook, James's car was already under police surveillance as he executed Rees's plan. He was filmed by CIB officers planting cocaine in her car which was later substituted for fake powder by the surveillance team.

A colleague of DC Tom Kingston's on the South East Regional Crime Squad, Detective Constable Austin Warnes, was to act as Rees's conduit to the Met. Warnes provided his superior, a Detective Inspector Latham, with the evidence against Kim James that had allegedly been obtained from a reliable but in fact entirely bogus informant referred to as "Tommy Mack".

DC Austin Warnes was later revealed as a corrupt police officer of the lowest order. He was described as both a "cocaine addict" and as "a sexual deviant". He was said to have supplied his own drug habit by stealing cocaine seized in raids in which he had been involved. In his article for *The Guardian* newspaper on 17th December 2000, journalist Tony Thompson, claimed that Warnes also colluded with *"professional criminals in the south London area to* [help them] *avoid capture and evade charges by providing them with information about police investigations. In order to cover himself and not face questioning about why he was accessing police files, Warnes would say one of his informants had knowledge relevant to the* case."

Thompson also went on to write: *"Warnes would regularly brag about fitting people up and applying pressure to ensnare people. He would carry out surveillance before making arrests to ensure they were carried out in the most compromising position possible. If a villain had a mistress, he would be arrested at her address rather than at home in order to increase the level of hassle if he pleaded not guilty. If he had a small child, the raid would take place late on Friday evening and fake drugs would be planted in his wife's possessions."*

"This would lead to the wife being held in custody and the child being taken into care over the weekend. By the end of the weekend, it would all be looking so grim he'd have to plead guilty. He said he collected fag ends - you can get DNA from traces of saliva - to plant at crime scenes to implicate people he didn't like."

During DC Warnes's subsequent Old Bailey trial, another frequently used scam was revealed. This one involved fake informants, who would be recruited by officers such as Warnes and then credited with providing information leading to an arrest. The "informant" would receive any reward money due and then split it with the detective concerned.

Following the planting of the drugs by Jimmy Cook, CIB officers decided that the best course of action was for DI Latham to pretend to acquiesce in Rees's plan and to therefore allow time for the anti-corruption team to gather all the evidence they needed to bring convictions against the plotters. Warrants were obtained and Kim James's home and car were searched. She was arrested, and without being informed that her arrest was merely a charade.

Warnes took a well-earned break in Portugal, oblivious to the net closing in around him. Simon James informed Social Services of his ex-wife's unfortunate predicament and prepared to take custody of his son. Roy Clark's "ghost squad" overheard a telephone conversation in which James made arrangements with Rees to make the final payment for Rees's services. However, before payment could be made, Kim James was released without charge.

By September 1999, the Met's anti-corruption squad had accumulated enough evidence against Rees and his co-conspirators to make a solid prosecution. Operation Two Bridges was called to a premature halt. A number of properties were raided in connection with evidence that had been gathered over the preceding six months. Twelve people were arrested including Rees, James, Warnes, and Cook.

Austin Warnes's bogus "informant" was also arrested and turned out to be none other than "celebrity gangster" and best-selling author Dave Courtney. Courtney claimed that he knew nothing of the plot to frame Kim James and, far from being an informant, he had a longstanding corrupt relationship with Warnes whereby Warnes was selling him information pertaining to police activity which he then passed on to his underworld associates. Courtney was cleared of all charges connected to the Kim James case. Indeed he boasted that he had stood in the dock on no less than ten separate occasions and on each one of them had been found not guilty. Following his acquittal, he made a statement: *"I always had faith in the British justice system. That not guilty verdict was both for the charge I faced and the accusation I was a grass. I have never been an informer."*

In December 2000, Jonathan Rees was finally jailed, but not for the murder of Daniel Morgan. He was sentenced at the Old Bailey to 6 years for conspiracy to pervert the course of justice. Simon James was likewise sentenced to 6 years on the same charge, and DC Warnes to 4 years. James Cook, just as Courtney had been, was acquitted. Rees's sentence was later increased to 7 years on appeal.

Rees was released from prison in May 2004, and such was his value to the *News of the World* that by the following year he had been re-hired by the tabloid on an estimated salary of around £150,000. By now, Andy Coulson was editor of the paper. He had been deputy editor to Rebekah Brooks in 2000 as the Kim James case had unfolded in court and in the national media. Coulson had also been deputy editor when Bob Quick had delivered his report into Operation Two Bridges naming *News of the World* executive editor Alex Marunchak among journalists who had been drawn to CIB3's attention during the covert surveillance of Rees's offices in Thornton Heath.

Despite this it appears that Coulson was oblivious to Rees's dubious background. Either that or he was unaware that Rees was accounting for such a substantial portion of his newspaper's wage bill.

In fact, Nick Davies wrote in *The Guardian* on 11th March 2011, shortly after Coulson's resignation from his government post: *"And yet the man who became the prime minister's media adviser, Andy Coulson, has always maintained in evidence to parliament and on oath in court that he knew nothing of any illegal activity during the seven years he spent at the top of the News of the World. The entire story unfolded without ever catching his eye. In the same way, the prime minister and his deputy were happy to appoint Coulson last May to oversee the communication between the British government and its people, even though they were already fully aware of all the essential facts."*

It seems astonishing that Coulson could be so blissfully unaware of the activities and practices that were everyday being carried out by his staff. Unfortunately for him, the Old Bailey jury thought so too. In July 2014, he was sentenced to 18 months in prison.

5

Dave Cook, Jacqui Hames and the Fourth Investigation

Owing to the unfortunate collapse of Operation Two Bridges and a further examination of the case by the Murder Review Group (MRG) who believed that they had identified *"new investigative opportunities"*, a fourth investigation into Daniel Morgan's murder was launched in 2002. Codenamed Operation Abelard, it too began as a covert operation and was this time overseen by Deputy Assistant Commissioner Andy Hayman.

The launch of the overt phase of the investigation was to be announced by Detective Chief Superintendent Dave Cook on the BBC television programme *Crimewatch* along with an appeal for information. However, in the days leading up to Cook's appearance on the show, which was scheduled for 26th June 2002, intelligence was received that Cook himself had become the subject of a surveillance operation. Two vans were seen parked outside his home from which the occupants could be seen taking photographs of Cook and his family. In the following days, DCS Cook found himself being continually followed. Noticing a faulty tail light on one of the vehicles, he reported it to the local police in Surrey and requested that the driver be apprehended. When officers stopped the van they found, to their astonishment, that it was being driven by Bradley Page who was an employee of the *News of the World* and a photographer for their foremost investigative reporter, Mazher Mahmood. The vans were leased to News International.

When then *News of the World* editor, Rebekah Brooks was asked about her newspaper's investigation into Cook, she claimed that they suspected he was having an affair with *Crimewatch* presenter and fellow serving police officer, Jacqui Hames. Brooks was to later repeat this extraordinary claim to the Leveson inquiry. Her explanation for her paper's investigation was extraordinary for one simple reason: Cook and Hames were married to each other and had been so for four years. They had been in a relationship for the previous 11 years. They had two children, and had even posed together for photographs that were later published in *Hello!* magazine. They had a joint bank account: a fact that would not have escaped the attention of the *News of the World's* army of "blaggers" and "specialist" investigators.

Detective Chief Superintendent Dave Cook: The only police officer the Morgan family trusted

Cook and Hames's marital status was no secret. As Alastair Morgan later commented, a simple Google search would have revealed that the couple were married. It certainly didn't warrant the full investigative resources of Britain's biggest newspaper.

Former Metropolitan Police Assistant Commissioner John Yates later said of Cook, in an article he wrote for *The Independent* newspaper in May 2013: *"He led the case from 2002 and did more than anyone to bring the right people to justice. A feisty and outspoken individual, he was also an extremely able and committed detective. Most importantly, he won the trust and respect of the family. Disturbingly, he provides an astonishing link between Southern Investigations, the News of the World and phone-hacking when, in July 2011, it was revealed that the paper had used the detective agency to tail Det Ch Supt Cook and his wife at the height of his involvement in leading the murder investigation."*

Yates, a former head of UK counter-terrorism, resigned from the Met in July 2011 at the height of the phone hacking scandal. This followed his report to the Commons Select Committee as early as 2009 that, following the convictions of *News of the World* employees Clive Goodman and Glenn Mulcaire for hacking into the voicemails of the royal family, *"there remain now insufficient grounds or evidence to arrest or interview anyone else and... no additional evidence has come to light."* These comments were made despite the Met having, by then, accumulated a *"vast"* amount of evidence against News International and its employees. Mr Yates was also understood to have been instrumental in the recruitment of Neil Wallis to a high profile public relations role within the Met, as indeed was the Met's Director of Public Affairs, Dick Fedorcio. Wallis was another former News International employee who was later to face charges relating to phone hacking. In calling for Yates's resignation, Member of Parliament Chris Bryant described the affair as having a *"very dirty smell"*.

Although he admits that there were huge failings in the Met's initial handling of the phone hacking inquiry, there has never been any suggestion of impropriety on the part of Mr Yates. Announcing his resignation on 18th July 2012, he made the following statement: *"Sadly, there continues to be a huge amount of inaccurate, ill-informed and on occasion downright malicious gossip published about me personally. This has the potential to be a significant distraction in my current role as the national lead for counter terrorism. I see no prospect of this improving in the coming weeks and months as we approach one of the most important events in the history of the Metropolitan Police Service, the 2012 Olympic Games. The threats that we face in the modern world are such that I would never forgive myself if I was unable to give total commitment to the task of protecting London and the country during this period. I simply cannot let this situation continue."*

The real motives behind the *News of the World's* surveillance of DCS Cook and his family are believed to have been far more sinister than an investigation into their marital status. Jacqui Hames herself believed that it was intended to intimidate her and Cook and to undermine the police investigation into Daniel Morgan's murder.

Later, in a statement to the Leveson Inquiry, she said: *"I believe that the real reason for the News of the World placing us under surveillance was that suspects in the Daniel Morgan murder inquiry were using their association with a powerful and well-resourced newspaper to try to intimidate us and so attempt to subvert the investigation. These events left me distressed, anxious and needing counselling and contributed to the break-down of my marriage to David in 2010. Given the impact of these events, I would like to know why the police did not investigate why we came to be placed under surveillance by a newspaper like this."*

Indeed, police intelligence had intercepted a telephone call made by Sid Fillery, the former police officer who had previously been accused of tampering with evidence during the first Morgan investigation. He had called his friend Alex Marunchak at the *News of the World.* Fillery told Marunchak about Cook's involvement in the new investigation, even though it had not yet been made public. Marunchak had agreed "*to sort him* [Dave Cook] *out*".

Although the prime suspect in the Daniel Morgan murder case, Jonathan Rees, was still in prison for his part in the attempted framing of Kim James, according to Bryan Madagan, a former private investigator and associate of both Rees and Daniel Morgan, Marunchak was known to have paid regular visits to Rees in jail.

Marunchak approached *News of the World* news editor, Greg Miskiw, and asked him to authorise surveillance of Cook on the basis that he was having an affair with Hames. Miskiw, despite apparently harbouring some reservations regarding Marunchak's real motives, agreed to the investigation.

It was Greg Miskiw, incidentally who was responsible for one of the most infamous quotes of a journalistic generation when he told Charles Begley: *"That is what we do – we go out and destroy other people's lives."*

Former *News of the World* reporter Begley was the complainant in what was later to be dubbed Pottergate. During the hype surrounding the release of the first Harry Potter film in 2001 he was assigned by his editor Rebekah Brooks to be the newspaper's official Harry Potter correspondent and was required by her to dress up as the young wizard at all times.

He says that on September 11th, within hours of the terrorist attacks on the twin towers of New York's World Trade Centre, he was summoned to Ms Brooks's office and roundly rebuked for not being in costume. Deputy Editor Andy Coulson was also in the office and is alleged to have insisted that Begley attend the following morning's press conference in full costume.

Begley later wrote of the incident in the *Independent on Sunday*: *"While every other editor and journalist was polarised into reporting the cataclysmic events in the States, Ms Wade* [later Brooks] *demanded one of her reporters dress up as none other than the children's character Harry Potter."*

Mr Begley did not turn up for the press conference the following morning, the humiliation having broken his spirit, and the case ended up before an employment tribunal. Miskiw made his remark about destroying people's lives during a recorded telephone conversation in which he sympathetically attempted to persuade Begley to return to work.

During the very height of the phone hacking scandal in July 2011, the *Daily Mirror* reported that the *News of the World* may have hacked the phones of dead victims of the 9/11 attack. This allegation followed the claims of a former New York City police officer who said that while he was working as a private investigator in 2001, he was approached by the *News of the World* and asked to access the phone records of the victims and their families, particularly the British victims of the attack. The former cop told the *Mirror* that he had turned the job down because he knew how insensitive it would have been and how bad it would have looked.

Greg Miskiw passed the investigation into Dave Cook and Jacqui Hames onto a private investigator who possessed no such reservations. A former non-league footballer, Glenn Mulcaire was later to find himself at the very epicentre of one of Britain's biggest ever scandals when, in January 2007, he was imprisoned for six months for hacking into the private voicemails of Prince William and other members of the royal family. The *News of the World's* royal correspondent, Clive Goodman, was also found guilty of the same charge and jailed for four months.

Although this wasn't the first reported incident of phone hacking, it was the first to be properly investigated. The lofty status of its royal victims left the Met with no alternative other than to mount a thorough investigation. Had Glenn Mulcaire not been clumsy enough to be discovered hacking the voicemails of the future king of England, the whole scandal could have been averted.

The *News of the World* maintained that Goodman had acted independently and that nobody else at the paper knew anything of such matters. Apparently shocked and horrified by the scandal, Andy Coulson resigned as editor. It appears that the Met, including

Assistant Commissioner Yates, were satisfied that Goodman had merely been a "rogue employee", and this despite huge amounts of evidence to the contrary having been gathered during the investigation into Mulcaire.

When it was revealed by the *Guardian* in 2011 that Mulcaire had also hacked the voicemails of missing schoolgirl Milly Dowler in 2002, again on behalf of the *News of the World*, his notoriety deepened and, in July 2014, he was sentenced to a further six months. It was by examining documents that had been seized during raids on Mulcaire's offices in August 2006 that Metropolitan police officers were able to identify over 4,000 potential victims of phone hacking that he had perpetrated on behalf of the *News of the World* alone.

Mulcaire, himself, says of the surveillance operation against Detective Chief Superintendent Dave Cook and his family that it would have been immediately apparent to his investigators that the couple were married from their joint bank account details, information that would have been easily accessible to a man of Mulcaire's talents. According to the notes he made at the time, "*no affair features*" and that it has all the hallmarks of a financial investigation.

In a bizarre case of role-reversal, it seems that the *News of the World* were now investigating senior police officers on behalf of the suspects in the criminal case that they were themselves investigating.

Jacqui Hames sheds more light on this when she referred to Mulcaire's notebooks in her statement to Leveson: "*In May 2011 police officers from Operation Weeting contacted me and informed me that my details had been found in Glenn Mulcaire's notebooks. I was then shown details of investigations undertaken by the News of the World into David and I back in 2002, which I had had no idea were going on at the time. The information that I was shown in the notebooks included detail such as my payroll and warrant numbers, the name of the police section house that I lived in when I first joined the police in 1977, the name, location and telephone number of my place of work in 2002, my and David's full home address and mobile phone number and some notes about my previous husband and his work details. The notes also contained notes about David, including his name, telephone number, rank and reference to "appeal" which I presume to be a reference to his appeal for information on Crimewatch. The date at the top of the notes was 3 July 2002, a week or so before the News of the World vans began to appear outside our home. This demonstrates to me that the News of the World knew full well that I was married to David at the time of the surveillance and thus gives the lie to their explanation for it."*

Detective Constable Jacqui Hames (front left) with fellow presenters on the set of the BBC's *"Crimewatch"* programme: Jill Dando, Nick Ross and David Hatcher (Photo: BBC)

Once the *News of the World's* interest in DCS

Cook had been brought to the attention of Cook and his team, detectives from Operation Abelard began to look more closely at the relationship between that newspaper and Southern Investigations. They discovered evidence that linked Rees and Fillery to Alex Marunchak that went back to at least 1987, the year of Daniel Morgan's murder. Armed with this evidence, the team made an application to the Met's Directorate of Professional Standards to request an urgent investigation into the relationship between Southern Investigations and the *News of the World.*

The DPS declined to take any action. Shortly after the application was submitted, in August 2002, Rebekah Brooks and her actor husband Ross Kemp met with Metropolitan Police Commissioner Sir John Stevens and his wife for dinner at the Ivy Club. The two couples were joined at a subsequent dinner by the Met's Director of Public Affairs Dick Fedorcio. Fedorcio, it should be pointed out, was later brought before the Leveson Inquiry in March 2012 to answer questions relating to his relationship with News International where, through his relationship with the then Miss Wade, he was able to secure work experience placements for both his own son and the son of Metropolitan Police Commissioner Sir Ian Blair.

Although the threat posed by the *News of the World* and their investigators was considered sufficient enough for Cook and his family to be provided with round-the-clock police protection, still no action was taken by the Met against the *News of the World* surveillance team. On 9th January 2003, Detective Chief Superintendent Cook confronted Brooks at New Scotland Yard where she was to be a guest at a drinks reception hosted by Commissioner Stevens. Also present were Commander Andre Baker and Dick Fedorcio. The meeting had been arranged by Fedorcio at the request of Commander Baker. Fedorcio later told Lord Leveson: *"It wasn't about taking any action against the News of the World; it was to help Mr Cook understand and come to terms with what had gone on."* He went on to describe the meeting as *"a welfare meeting"* on behalf of DCS Cook, and that Baker had merely been *"looking after a member of his staff."*

In late 2002, as head of the Met's Serious Crime (Homicide) Directorate, Commander Baker was also involved in the investigation into the abduction and murder of Milly Dowler. Had Baker known then that the very same *News of the World* employees were also responsible for hacking into the teenager's voicemails and undermining that investigation too, it seems inconceivable that his meeting with the newspaper's editor would have passed off quite so amicably.

However, following this meeting, Rebekah Brooks did promise that she would look into the matter. The following day she met with *News of the World* Managing Editor Stuart Kuttner to discuss the issue of the possible subversion by *News of the World* staff of the Daniel Morgan murder investigation. Also on the agenda was Alex Marunchak, now a high ranking member of News International's management team, and his highly dubious relationship with Cook's prime suspect Jonathan Rees who was currently serving a prison sentence for conspiracy to pervert the course of justice.

It is alleged that also at that meeting with Kuttner and Brooks was the newspaper's Deputy Editor, Andy Coulson. The same Andy Coulson who had been promoted to Editor by the time of Rees's release from prison three years later and subsequent recruitment by the paper. Indeed, this was the same Andy Coulson who later told the Leveson Inquiry that he had absolutely no knowledge of Rees or of his criminal activities. This is the same Andy Coulson who was to become a senior member of the British Prime Minister's Downing Street staff. Less than a fortnight after this meeting took place, Brooks had been moved to *The Sun* and Coulson had replaced her as Editor of the *News of the World*.

It was during Operation Abelard that the offices of

Southern Investigations in Grange Road, Thornton Heath were raided and Sid Fillery's computer was seized. Although police found nothing on it to connect Fillery to the Morgan killing, they did find 106 references to the *News of the World* and 97 mentions of Alex Marunchak. Unknown to them at the time, the Met had taken the first step in what was to become the notorious phone hacking scandal.

One email appeared to be reporting back to Marunchak regarding the burglary of a prominent person on behalf of the *News of the World*. In the email, Fillery described it as a *"sortie into the address of the woman concerning Ascot."* The police interpretation was that Southern Investigations had *"gained unauthorised access into a private domestic property with a view to gaining information on the resident."*

Following these revelations, a number of public figures, including the actor Hugh Grant, also came forward to claim that they had been the victims of similar break-ins where nothing had been stolen. Derek Haslam, who worked undercover at Southern Investigations for the Met's anti-corruption unit, later confirmed that the agency had routinely burgled addresses in an attempt to *"obtain embarrassing information for the newspaper"*.

In a classic case of poacher turning gamekeeper, Detective Constable Haslam had been passing information to CIB3 since the 1980s. In 1988 he had been posted to Norbury police station, long suspected of being a hotbed of corruption. Also based at Norbury was Detective Duncan Hanrahan, later jailed for 9 years for his part in extensive and wide-ranging corrupt police practises.

It was Haslam who had exposed the web of corruption that shadowed the supposed suicide of Alan "Taffy" Holmes. Haslam also reported to his CIB handlers that Hanrahan was known to be passing illegally gathered information on to Commander Ray Adams. Whilst stationed at Norbury, he also claims to have discovered a handwritten death threat on his desk.

As a well-connected Met detective and an old acquaintance of Jonathan Rees, Haslam was to easily find employment at Southern Investigations when he "left" the police service in 1998. But unbeknown to Rees and Fillery, he was still reporting back to anti-corruption officers at CIB3 and continued to do so until his cover was blown by Rees's 2006 arrest for Daniel Morgan's murder.

When Haslam was quoted in the *London Evening Standard* in 2012 alleging that Southern Investigations had burgled the properties of celebrities and politicians in an effort to discover embarrassing stories for their paymasters at the *News of the World* it made headline news and fanned the flames of the phone hacking scandal that was already engulfing Fleet Street.

Labour MP, Tom Watson, who in 2009 was himself a victim of a burglary where private documents had been rifled through but nothing taken, made the following comment: *"News Corporation in the UK stands accused of phone hacking, computer hacking, bribery, conspiring to pervert the course of justice, inappropriate covert surveillance, lies and cover-up. Now added to the list is the allegation of burglary."*

The computer forensics team attached to Operation Abelard, however, weren't satisfied with the examination of Fillery's email account and other computer files that intrinsically linked Southern Investigations with Marunchak and the *News of the World*. They also discovered pornographic material on his hard drive and evidence that Fillery had searched for, and downloaded from the internet, images of child pornography.

For this, Fillery was convicted in October 2003. Pleading guilty to 13 counts of making indecent images of children at Bow Street Magistrates Court, he expressed his remorse and humiliation. The court heard that he had made *"a planned and conscious decision to access unambiguously named websites."*

Passing sentence, District Judge Caroline Tubbs, added the case had given her *"a great deal of concern."* Fillery received a three-year community rehabilitation order.

As Detective Chief Superintendent Cook's murder inquiry gathered pace, Glenn Vian's house was bugged and so was a car belonging to a second suspect. The police spent £245,000 buying the house next door to Vian's in Orchard Road, South Croydon where they installed surveillance equipment. They drilled through the walls to plant listening devices. From here they could monitor every conversation Vian had.

As a result of their covert operation, the investigating team were convinced that they had accumulated enough evidence to link their suspects to Daniel Morgan's murder and that they would, at last, be able to make the charges stick. Jonathan Rees, who was still in jail for his part in the Kim James case, was once more charged with murder. Seven further suspects were arrested and later bailed, including the Vian brothers, and in March 2003 files were submitted to the CPS for consideration.

In early September, the Crown Prosecution Service announced that they did not believe there was sufficient evidence to mount a successful prosecution and all eight suspects were released from their bail obligations. In light of the CPS's decision, the MRG concluded that *"all avenues of inquiry had been exhausted"*.

6

Sir Ian Blair, Gary Eaton and the Failed Prosecution

Sir Ian Blair was born in Chester in 1953 and educated at The Wrekin College in Shropshire. The old school moto was *"Either to conquer or to die"*, and included among their alumni former manager of The Beatles, Brian Epstein. Blair later graduated from Oxford University in 1974 and joined the Met as part of their High Potential Developer Scheme for Graduates. His rise through the police ranks was rapid. By 1985 he had made Detective Inspector, and in February 2005, succeeded Sir John Stevens as Commissioner.

Unfortunately for Blair, his tenure as Britain's most senior policeman lasted only three years. He became the first Commissioner of the Met to resign from office since James Munro in 1890 who had clashed with then Home Secretary Henry Matthews over police pay and conditions. Although a highly respected detective, Munro had also failed to apprehend the notorious Jack the Ripper. Many years later it was alleged that Munro had been convinced that he knew the identity of the Ripper but had been forced into keeping his suspicions quiet.

A champion of the Labour government, Blair was unpopular amongst the Conservative held London Assembly and the incoming Mayor of London Boris Johnson made it a priority to dispense with his services. In only his first day as Chairman of the Metropolitan Police Authority, Johnson called a meeting on 1st October 2008 at which, according to Richard Edwards writing in *The Telegraph*, there was a heated exchange during the course of which Sir Ian asked the Mayor if he had his backing. *"Mr Johnson responded 'you certainly do not have my full confidence'".*

The following day, Sir Ian announced his

resignation to a televised news conference, saying that *"without the mayor's backing I do not think I can continue in the job."* He offered his resignation to Home Secretary Jacqui Smith who accepted it with genuine regret. Johnson's take on proceedings had a slightly different perspective. He announced that: *"Following a meeting with Sir Ian yesterday, he has agreed to give someone else the chance to offer new leadership for policing in London. And I am sure he has done the right thing."* He even went on to thank Blair for his *"lasting and distinguished contribution to policing"*. Most telling was Mr Johnson's assertion that there was *"no particular story or allegation that was uppermost in our considerations."* In fact, at the time of Sir Ian Blair's resignation from office, the Met were in crisis over one such particular story and that was the shooting dead of 27-year-old Brazilian electrician Jean Charles de Menezes three years earlier.

Mayor of London Boris Johnson meets Metropolitan Police Commissioner Sir Ian Blair

Unknown to Mr de Menezes, and by an unfortunately fatal coincidence, he lived in a flat in the same block as suspected Islamist terrorist, Hussain Osman. Osman was suspected of being involved in a failed attempt to detonate a suicide bomb on the London Underground on 21st July 2005, shortly after a wave of similar attacks had devastated the capital just two weeks earlier. After a gym membership card was discovered by police in a back-pack that had failed to detonate, they were led to an address in Scotia Road, Tulse Hill. Osman was later arrested in Rome and sentenced to forty years for his part in the plot.

On the morning of 22nd July, the building in Scotia Road where both Osman and Jean Charles de Menezes lived was under heavy police surveillance. The plan was for armed officers to stop anyone who left the building and to question them at a discrete distance in the hope of unearthing more intelligence on their target.

When Jean Charles left his home that morning to go to work, there were no armed officers available and no one trained in questioning suspects. To make matters worse the surveillance team had not been shown, nor had they in their possession, a quality photograph of their target. All they had seen was the faded passport style photograph on the gym membership card earlier that morning at a 5am briefing. This shouldn't have been a problem because the Met had a video camera stationed in a van that was parked in the street outside the flats. Residents and visitors were filmed as they left the building and their images fed back to the Met's control room. Unfortunately, as Jean Charles walked past the surveillance van, the officer charged with taking video images, codenamed "Frank", was not at his post but was answering the call of nature.

Surveillance officers from SO12 began to pursue Jean Charles on foot with the growing suspicion that the man they were following was actually Hussain Osman. However, they failed to apprehend him before he boarded the number 2 bus to Brixton tube station. They were forced to follow him onto the bus. Upon reaching his destination, Jean Charles then made the decision that, in all likelihood, cost him his life. He disembarked the bus and then, on realising that the station was closed, hopped back on in order to travel on to Stockwell Station. Recognising this as a common diversionary tactic, the surveillance officers were now convinced that they had their man. The de Menezes family lawyer, Michael Mansfield QC, later told the inquest into Jean Charles's death that this decision alone meant that he was *"virtually dead"*.

On arrival at Stockwell, Jean Charles headed for the station. Officers were ordered by Gold Commander Cressida Dick, who was in overall charge of the operation in the control room, to stop him boarding a train *"at all costs"*. The officers involved later denied that they ever received the instruction to stop Jean Charles entering the station, something that they would have been able to do. Officers also attributed the weak radio signal inside the station as contributing to the confusion. The armed officers who shot de Menezes claim that they heard a surveillance officer tell them over the radio *"this is definitely our man"*. The surveillance officer concerned denies that he ever made such a statement.

In the aftermath of the shooting, police sources claimed that Jean Charles de Menezes was acting suspiciously and that he ran into the station and vaulted the ticket barriers. Some police reports even suggested that he was wearing a heavily padded jacket with wires hanging from it. The Met also claimed at the time that the CCTV cameras at the station were not functioning correctly on the morning in question. This was untrue. Security footage that was supressed at the time has since been made public and clearly shows de Menezes calmly strolling into the station blissfully unaware of the deadly police operation unfolding in his wake not more than fifteen feet away. He is seen stopping to check the time of his train and then again to pick up a *Metro* newspaper. He passes through the ticket barrier and is seen to be wearing a light denim jacket with the buttons undone and revealing a dark pullover. There are no wires hanging from his person and he has no back-pack or bag of any kind.

Armed officers are then seen vaulting the barriers behind him and following de Menezes down the escalator towards the station platforms. On boarding the train, the two armed officers were directed by a surveillance officer who was already stationed in de Menezes's carriage. *"He is here,"* he told them, and pointed to Menezes as he sat reading his newspaper, still unaware of what was happening around him.

At this point, the armed officers claim that they clearly shouted a warning: *"Armed police!"* but the suspect ignored this warning, stood up and began to approach them. They claim that they had no choice but to kill him. However, there were six witnesses also in that carriage that morning and each of them has testified under oath that no such warning was given and that Jean Charles de Menezes did not approach the officers. Instead, they say that as de Menezes stood up, the surveillance officer pinned him back in his seat and the two armed officers shot him seven times in the head from point-blank range. One of the witnesses even said of the armed officers: *"We had no idea whether they were police or terrorists."*

The following day, Sir Ian Blair appeared on national television to give a statement in which he said that the shooting was *"directly linked to the ongoing and expanding anti-terrorist operation."* He also re-asserted Scotland Yard's discredited claims *"that the man was challenged and refused to obey police instructions."*

Following the shooting on 22nd July, police officers at the scene lost no time in positively identifying Jean Charles de Menezes and in realising that they had made a tragic mistake. But, in Sir Ian's statement on the 23rd there was no mention of this and no official apology was forthcoming. The de Menezes family later claimed that Sir Ian shouldered the *"responsibility for the lies told about Jean and the cover-up by police."* On hearing of his resignation as Metropolitan Police Commissioner in October 2008, they said: *"Ian Blair should have resigned three years ago when he and his men killed the wrong man."*

Some conspiracy theorists believe that Jean Charles de Menezes was deliberately executed because, as an electrician working on the London Underground, he had inadvertently stumbled upon a government plot, but the reasoning behind such claims are, at best, extremely vague. Whatever the truth of the matter, the certainty is that this unfortunate incident was another nail in the coffin of Sir Ian Blair's erstwhile impressive police career.

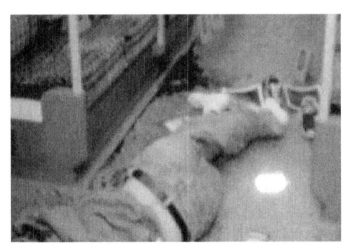

Jean Charles de Menezes lies dead in a blood stained carriage

In April 2006, Commissioner Blair had chaired a top secret meeting of his senior management team at which the decision was made to review the evidence in the Daniel Morgan murder case. Operation Abelard II was launched on the basis that the first investigation into Morgan's death involving Detective Sergeant Sid Fillery and other officers from Catford police station had been *"compromised"*.

Barely had the meeting been adjourned when the news of the forthcoming investigation had already found its way to the main suspects in the case, including Jonathan Rees and Fillery himself. A police intelligence report on Rees suggested that Alex Marunchak of the *News of the World* had confirmed a leak from what he referred to as Blair's *"inner sanctum"*. By now, Sir Ian's predecessor, Sir John Stevens, was on the *News of the World's* payroll as a columnist; so too was Rees following his release from prison twelve months earlier. Indeed, on his release from prison, Rees had been overheard boasting that he had planned to make *"an awful lot of money"* out of his connection to Alex Marunchak whom police intelligence reported Rees as describing as *"still highly thought of by Murdoch and can do no wrong."*

It should be pointed out that, contrary to Rees's assertion, when asked by MP Tom Watson during his appearance before the House of Commons Select Committee in 2011, Mr Murdoch completely denied knowing Marunchak. The transcript reads:

Mr Watson: *"Finally, can I ask you, when did you first meet Mr Alex Marunchak?"*
Rupert Murdoch: *"Mister-?"*
Mr Watson: *"Alex Marunchak. He worked for the company for 25 years."*
Rupert Murdoch: *"I don't remember meeting him. I might have shaken hands walking through the office, but I don't have any memory of him."*

Jonathan Rees's association with the *News of the World* would eventually outlast that of both Marunchak and editor, Andy Coulson. The newspaper only ended their relationship with him when he was charged with Daniel Morgan's murder for the second time, in 2008, twenty-one years after he was first arrested for the same crime.

Detective Chief Superintendent Dave Cook was once more appointed to lead the inquiry into Morgan's death. And, once more, staff at the *News of the World* prepared to undermine Cook's investigation. By the summer of 2006, a story regarding Jacqui Hames' business interests was already circulating Fleet Street. The originators of the story were said to be Alex Marunchak and Jonathan Rees. Journalist Peter Jukes writes: *"Derek Haslam claims that Rees asked him to call the Inland Revenue to discover financial details about a previous partner of Jacqui Hames in 2003. He never did this but neither was any warning ever passed on from his reports to Cook or Hames despite the fact they were both still serving police officers."*

News International were never to forgive Dave Cook for his dogged pursuit of justice in the Daniel Morgan murder case. Morgan's brother Alastair who had been vocal in his criticism of the general mishandling of the case by the police, said of Cook that he was *"the only policeman we ever trusted."*

Early one January morning in 2012, Cook himself was arrested following an IPCC raid on his Berkshire home. A statement by the Independent Police Complaints Commission at the time read: *"A 52-year-old man, a former Met officer, was arrested by the IPCC at his home in Berkshire this morning on suspicion of misconduct in public office and Data Protection Act offences. The arrest is the result of information passed to the IPCC by the Metropolitan Police Service team investigating Operation Elveden and relates to the alleged passing of unauthorised information to a journalist."*

But this doesn't tell the whole story. In what appears to be a blatant misuse of their own self-regulatory body, it was News International's US-based Management and Standards Committee that passed information regarding Cook to Met officers investigating police corruption as part of Operation Elveden. His "crime" was to have shared information with the *Sun's* then crime correspondent Mike Sullivan regarding the fifth Daniel Morgan investigation. There was never any suggestion that Cook ever received payment for this information and Sullivan was never even questioned. As lead investigator in the case it would have been Cook's responsibility to liaise with the media anyway and, from time to time, plant stories in the press in order to maintain public interest in the case as more information was sought.

Indeed, because of the web of police corruption that already surrounded the Morgan case, Cook was positively encouraged by his commanding officer, Deputy Assistant Commissioner John Yates, to engage with the press and to conduct the investigation with as much transparency as possible.

The timing of Cook's arrest could not have been more fortuitous for News International. It came on the eve of his appearance before the Leveson Inquiry where he was to be a key witness. He had been expected to give evidence against News International following his experiences at the hands of Glen Mulcaire and their surveillance team during the fourth Morgan investigation in 2002. Referring to Cook's arrest, Dominic Ponsford wrote in the *Press Gazette* that *"...one does not have to be a conspiracy theorist to suspect that the motive was to silence him and others who might be tempted to follow his example."* In the event, Cook's former wife and fellow detective, Jacqui Hames, stood before Lord Leveson and gave an explosive account of her own experiences; experiences she later likened, whilst talking to Channel 4 News, to being *"hunted"*.

On November 10th 2015 the IPCC announced that it would not be in the public interest to proceed against Dave Cook who was cleared of all charges. On the same day, Peter Jukes summed the affair up in his *Byline* column: *"That Cook should have been gagged for four years on such a slender charge, on information disclosed for such obviously self-interested reasons by a company under criminal investigation, is a further abomination in a long list of injustices around Britain's most investigated murder."*

In 2005, Dave Cook was assembling his team for the forthcoming fifth investigation. Because of long-standing concerns connecting the prime suspects in the case with Masonic Lodge membership, detectives appointed to the team were required to state that they were not, nor ever had been, Freemasons. Alastair Morgan's constituency representative on the London Assembly, Jennette Arnold, described the case as *"a reminder of the old police culture of corruption and unaccountability"*. DCS Cook, himself, said of Daniel Morgan's murder that it was *"one of the worst-kept secrets in south-east London"* and that *"a whole cabal of people"* knew the identities of those responsible. He also dismissed several urban myths that had surfaced in the years following the murder.

For instance, there was talk that Morgan may have been killed by a jealous husband or a disgruntled client. Another rumour was that Morgan had been executed because of his involvement with a Columbian drugs cartel. Cook poured cold water on all of these theories, insisting that the suspects were all *"white Anglo-Saxons"*. The one motive that seems to stand the test of time is that Morgan was hawking a story about police corruption around Fleet Street and was silenced before he could sell it.

Once more, bugs were planted in the homes and business premises of the suspects and further evidence was gradually gathered. By August 2006, officers of Operation Abelard II were satisfied that they had enough evidence to press charges and began to make arrests. The supposition was that Jonathan Rees had arranged Morgan's murder and had lured him to the Golden Lion in Sydenham in the knowledge that his friend, Sid Fillery, and other close associates from Catford police station would be on the investigating team. Rees ensured that he was seen to leave the pub prior to the attack. Meanwhile Garry and Glenn Vian were driven to the car park at the rear of the Golden Lion by another man, Jimmy

Cook. Cook remained in the car preparing for a quick getaway and as Garry Vian acted as a lookout Glenn Vian struck the fatal blows to Morgan's head.

The Vian brothers were the first arrested and then bailed pending further inquiries. At the time, Garry Vian was already serving a 14 year sentence for attempting to smuggle millions of pounds worth of class A drugs into the UK. The drugs had been hidden in pianos and Vian had been described in court as a drug dealer on a "commercial" scale. Jimmy Cook was arrested the following month. He too was bailed. Incidentally, this was the same Jimmy Cook who had been filmed by undercover officers in 2000 planting cocaine in Kim James's Fiat Punto at the behest of Jonathan Rees. In April 2008, Garry and Glenn Vian, and Jimmy Cook answered bail and, along with Rees, were all charged with the murder of Daniel Morgan. Sid Fillery was also arrested and charged with perverting the course of justice for his role in sabotaging the first Morgan murder investigation. He was also accused of threatening a potential witness in the case; a witness who later turned out to be Gary Eaton.

A serving police constable from Southwark was also arrested on suspicion of misconduct in a public office. He had allegedly been passing sensitive information about the investigation to Rees and his fellow suspects. He was never charged and resigned from the Met before disciplinary action could be brought against him. But this clearly illustrates how deep Rees and Fillery's influence still was in the Met and how easy it was for them to gather information. It has been said of Rees that he once followed likely targets, collecting the cigarette ends that they dropped, and then threatened to have them planted at a crime scene by his friends in the Met. This would often be a rape scene. The subject, fearful of implication in a serious crime due to the presence of their DNA, would completely submit to Rees's will and provide him with the information he required.

A provisional trial date was set for November 2010

but during the pre-trial hearings the case began to unravel. Perhaps the best explanation of how a £30m prosecution that had been three years in the building could so spectacularly have come to nothing can probably be found among the 147 page review of the investigation conducted jointly by the CPS and the MPS and published in May 2012 (a complete transcript of which can be found at the back of this book).

The prosecution case hinged on the testimony of three key witnesses, all of whom were "assisting offenders" whose handling was covered by the Serious Organised Crime and Police Act of 2005, otherwise known as SOCPA. In February 2010, the first of these witnesses, Gary Eaton, was found to be unreliable and dismissed. He had claimed that he had been offered a substantial amount of money to kill Daniel Morgan; an offer he had declined. The problem was that he also claimed that he had served in the Falklands War with the Royal Navy and with the United States Navy during the invasion of Panama, both of which claims were patently untrue.

Eaton also said that he had witnessed the aftermath of Danny Morgan's brutal killing and was expected to identify Glenn and Garry Vian as being present in the car park of the Golden Lion at the time. But during the hearing it was revealed that not only was Eaton a pathological liar with tendencies for extreme violence but also that he had been "prompted and coached" by lead investigator Dave Cook into implicating the Vian brothers. The judge, Mr Justice Maddison, described how Eaton had been taken by Cook to a secret location and left alone in a hotel room until he became distressed and "broke down". Half an hour later, Cook sent Eaton a text message that Cook later deleted from his phone. Subsequently Eaton changed his story and agreed to implicate Glenn and Garry Vian in Morgan's murder.

Cook continued to directly contact Eaton throughout the course of his investigation which contravened rules that a "sterile corridor" should be maintained between the investigating team and the witness whose independent police handlers were tasked with taking Eaton's witness statements and debriefing him. During the lengthy debriefing process, which lasted from August 2006 to December 2007, it was required that an appropriate adult should be present at all times because of Eaton's history of psychiatric problems. However, Eaton was reluctant to have anybody else present. The interviews went ahead anyway and this too was against guidelines.

Maddison also listed other failings in the handling of Gary Eaton. He and his girlfriend had been paid £72,000 as officers wrestled with his heavy drinking, erratic behaviour and threats of violence. He had a 28 year prison sentence reduced to just 3 years in return for testifying against the Vian brothers, a sentence that he had already served by the time the trial collapsed. He had been convicted of 51 crimes including conspiracy to murder, bribery, blackmail, drug smuggling and firearms offences, but Eaton walked away from it all and was given a new identity under the witness protection programme.

Despite all this, six months later Gary Eaton was the star witness as another high profile case collapsed. This time he claimed that he had been hired as a hitman by a woman called Mandy Fleming who wanted him to kill her wealthy husband. During the course of that trial, Eaton constantly referred to Fleming as Denise instead of Mandy. He could not remember the make of the gun that he had allegedly bought in order to carry out the hit, nor could he remember the address of the alleged target who he thought was Irish but, indeed, was not.

In dismissing Eaton's testimony, the judge in the Fleming case, Richard Hone, said that he was: *"not just unreliable but false and highly dangerous."* He also added: *"Eaton is capable of inventing detailed accounts of events which never happened and shows either blatant untruthfulness or alternatively a component of his personality disorder typified by folie de grandeur and self-aggrandisement. By the time the summing up of Eaton's evidence of unreliability, fabrication and fantasy had concluded it would be impossible to find a sufficient bedrock of truth upon which a jury could convict any of the defendants."*

Following Eaton's dismissal from the Morgan case, the CPS concluded that they had insufficient evidence to proceed against Sid Fillery and he was granted a stay of prosecution.

In November 2010, a second so-called supergrass was dismissed. Sally Ann Wood was the former girlfriend of alleged getaway driver Jimmy Cook. She had told police that Cook had confessed to her his role in the killing of Daniel Morgan and had described to her the events of the night of 10th March 1987. Her story confirmed the suspicions that the investigating officers on the case had long held regarding Morgan's murder.

But during the course of Wood's debriefing by her handlers, the body-count began to grow. She alleged that the Vian brothers had been involved in no less than twelve further murders, claiming that she had been present at one of them and had fired a shot into the victim's dead body. As the months passed, her claims became more outlandish. She declared knowledge of thirty murders and provided police with the names of victims and the locations where their bodies were buried in Epping Forest. Scotland Yard was forced to act, and set up a specialist unit to investigate her allegations. Her computer was examined and the alleged burial sites were excavated. No bodies were discovered. It was found that the names she had given to the police belonged to missing persons she had come across on the internet. With her credibility, not to mention her sanity, seriously undermined, Wood's evidence was ruled inadmissible by Mr Justice Maddison and Jimmy Cook was also acquitted. The evidence of both these witnesses was described in court as having being undermined by *"factors that adversely affected their credibility."*

Even more damaging to the prosecution case was their failure to disclose evidence to the defence. During the course of the previous 24 years, a staggering 750,000 pages of evidence relating to the Daniel Morgan murder had been amassed by the Met. Much of it had not been computerised, and much of it was poorly logged. It was barely possible for the prosecution to access all of the available evidence and unreasonable to expect the defence team to do the same.

When, in 2010, a further 18 crates of evidence were discovered in an abandoned storage facility, the crisis deepened. The prosecution was drowning in a sea of misplaced evidence. But worse was to come: contained within these crates was the revelation that DCS Cook's third witness, James Ward, had been a police informant since 1987 even though both Ward and the police had previously denied this. There was also evidence to suggest that Ward had a long-standing and sometimes corrupt relationship with senior officers in the drug squad. He was said to have paid one officer £50,000 in return for a reduced sentence.

Ward was a large scale drug smuggler who was known to the Vian brothers through their criminal activities. He and Garry Vian had both been sentenced to long term prison sentences in 2005 for drugs offences. Whilst in prison during 2006, Ward was approached by Detective Chief Superintendent Cook who was investigating the recently reopened Daniel Morgan case. In return for the promise of a reduced sentence, Ward told DCS Cook that Glenn Vian had confessed to him that he had been paid £20,000 to kill Daniel Morgan, and had also told him about the axe with which he used to carry out the attack. He said that Vian had boasted about what he had done: *"I done him straight in the head with an axe. He should have been wearing a crash helmet."*

The defence claimed that the Met had deliberately withheld the crates of evidence in order to conceal their previously corrupt relationship with their star witness. David Whitehouse QC told the court that Ward *"is a career criminal who has been able to remain active in crime by playing the informant – he has had relationships, including financial relationships with police officers. He has given information to the police, some of it true, some not true. The result is the police have been prepared to make representations to judges to seek lighter sentences when he is caught."*

As revelation followed revelation, Mr Justice Maddison dismissed Ward from the case and, according to Sandra Laville in *The Guardian*, "the relationship between the prosecution and the Morgan murder team dissolved into acrimony."

The death knell for both came in March 2011 when a further four crates of evidence were unearthed by chance just weeks before the trial was due to begin. The counsel for the prosecution was furious with the Met, and their relationship slipped further towards breaking point. The lead prosecutor for the CPS, Nicholas Hilliard QC, resignedly acknowledged that the police were unable to give assurances that all the available documented evidence had been made available to the defence and as such the remaining defendants could not be guaranteed a fair trial. Indeed, it seems unlikely that all of the evidence had been made available to the prosecution themselves. Laville concludes her article: *"The collapse of the costly and notorious investigation leaves a backlog of unanswered questions and accusations of institutionalised dishonesty. After tens of millions of pounds in public money, those who wielded the axe against Daniel Morgan can also rest in the knowledge that they will probably never be brought to justice."*

The trial had seen some of the longest running legal argument ever submitted in a British criminal court but on the 11th March 2011, 24 years and 1 day after Daniel Morgan's murder, the CPS formally dropped all charges against Jonathan Rees and his former brothers-in-law, Glenn and Garry Vian. In their review of the case, the CPS later stated: *"The main reason for the withdrawal of the prosecution was the Crown's inability to fully satisfy their disclosure obligations."*

The Morgan family were once more left bewildered. Although they expressed satisfaction with Dave Cook and his investigating team, they condemned the Mets failure to bring a prosecution in the case. In a statement, they claimed that during their 24-year campaign for justice, they had encountered *"stubborn obstruction and worse at the highest levels of the Metropolitan Police"*.

In his summing up of the hearing, Mr Justice Maddison praised the prosecution and said that it had been *"principled"* and *"right"* for them to drop the case. However, he also made it clear that the police had been right to bring the prosecution in the first place, saying that they had *"ample grounds to justify the arrest and prosecution of the defendants"*.

Detective Chief Superintendent Hamish Campbell, on behalf of the Met, apologised to the Morgan family and acknowledged that previous investigations had been tainted by police corruption. He said: *"This current investigation has identified, ever more clearly, how the initial inquiry failed the family and wider public. It is quite apparent that police corruption was a debilitating factor in that investigation."*

Campbell was an experienced and high-ranking homicide detective who had led the investigation into the Jill Dando shooting in 1999, unfortunately arresting and successfully prosecuting the wrong man. He later headed the 2011 review into the disappearance of three-year-old Madeleine McCann in Portugal in 2007, during which he was to say: *"Of course there is a possibility she is alive."* Campbell later took charge of Operation Yewtree, the investigation into claims of historic sexual abuse by Jimmy Savile and other celebrities. It is believed that Savile's victims numbered into the hundreds and possibly into the thousands and that he was responsible for committing 34 acts of rape.

Cressida Dick, Britain's highest ever ranking female police officer, had by March 2011 risen to the rank of Assistant Commissioner, a rank she attained following the shooting of Jean Charles Menezes by armed officers who were at the time under her command, and following the resignation of her predecessor John Yates in the wake of the phone hacking scandal. She issued a joint statement with the CPS in May 2012 regarding the joint review of the Daniel Morgan case: *"This case, as the trial judge said, was of an exceptional scale and complexity, with over three quarters of a million documents gathered over 20 years being examined. The issues around the disclosure exercise were such that we could not guarantee that all relevant material had been identified, considered and disclosed so as to ensure a fair trial. A further factor related to the unreliability of critical witnesses.*

"To this end, the purpose of the review was to identify potential good practice and learning for both police and prosecutors for future cases. What the review was not was an investigation into allegations of corruption; nor was it intended to serve the purpose of an investigation for police disciplinary purposes. Those recommendations identified within the review will now be implemented by both agencies."

On 22nd February 2017, Cressida Dick succeeded Bernard Hogan-Howe to become London's first female Police Commissioner. Predictably, her appointment did not pass without objections being raised, notably by the family of Jean Charles Menezes who wrote to London Mayor Sadiq Khan stressing that: *"We cannot be expected to accept that the most senior police officer in the country, a post that is expected to uphold the highest standards of professionalism, to command public confidence and ultimately be responsible for ensuring that no police officer acts with impunity, be filled by someone that is clearly tainted by her failure to live up to any of those requirements."*

But *The Guardian* newspaper gave a more positive

appraisal when Mary Dejevsky wrote regarding the new Commissioner's involvement in the tragic death of Mr Menezes: *"She will always have before her a salutary reminder of what can go wrong – whether because the overall atmosphere has not been properly appraised, because the orders given were not precise enough, or simply because insufficient account has been taken of the human factor. That knowledge, that awareness, must surely be a plus."*

"Individuals make mistakes for many reasons. But to treat a mistake as an automatic disqualification for advancement – even as heinous a mistake as presiding over a botched operation that resulted in the killing of an innocent man – could be depriving organisations, and the country, of leaders who have been tested and will not make the same mistake again."

For her own part Ms Dick described her appointment as the UK's senior police officer as being *"an extraordinary privilege"*, while Prime Minister Theresa May welcomed the news by saying Dick possessed *"the exceptional qualities needed to meet the challenge of leading the Met"* and added that *"she will be a champion of the most vulnerable who the police are there to protect"*.

Regarding the Daniel Morgan murder trial and the defendants' well-documented links to the *News of the World,* MP Tom Watson gave a damning speech to an adjournment debate at the House of Commons in which he stated: *"News of the World crime journalist Alex Marunchak was a close associate of Mr Morgan's business partner Mr Rees - who became a main suspect in his murder - and regularly paid his company Southern Investigations for information... Jonathan Rees and Sid Fillery were at the corrupt nexus of private investigators, police officers and journalists at the News of the World. Southern Investigations was the hub of police and media contacts involving the illegal theft and disclosure of information obtained through Rees and Fillery's corrupt contacts."*

Mr Watson went on to pass comment on the Dave

Cook/Jacqui Hames surveillance affair: *"When Detective Chief Inspector Dave Cook started to investigate the murder, at a time when Mr Rees was still a suspect, it is alleged Mr Marunchak placed the police officer under surveillance. The person who was investigating a murder was put under close surveillance by a close business associate of the man he was investigating."*

MP Tom Watson delivers a speech to parliament (Photo:PA)

In an interview he gave to journalist Kirsty Whalley only days after his acquittal, Glenn Vian spoke of how his life had been ruined by what he described as a *"24 year nightmare"*. He claimed that he had been at home looking after his children while his wife was out at work on the night of Daniel Morgan's murder. He told Ms Whalley, *"There were 63 witnesses in the Golden Lion pub and no one could put us there. All of the evidence was based on hearsay and second hand information. There was no forensic evidence, no ID and no fingerprints."*

Glenn and Garry Vian following their acquittal in 2011

He admitted to knowing his alleged victim well and had done some work for him and Jonathan Rees at Southern Investigations. He had even carried out building work at Morgan's home where he had met the dead man's wife and children. According to Vian he was shocked when he heard the news about Morgan's murder which was relayed to him from Rees via Vian's mother, Rees's mother-in-law.

Speaking of the surveillance operation that Dave Cook and his team carried out against him in 2002 and again in 2006, Vian said: *"I found a microphone in the back garden when I was pruning the ivy hedge in 2002. I had no idea we were being bugged. Once we found one, we figured there would be more. You would have thought if they have been bugging me for that long, if there was anything to prove I was a bad character, they would have it."*

In the article, published on 16th March 2011, Vian spoke of his time spent on remand in both Wandsworth and Belmarsh prisons and the hardships that his family were forced to endure. In all, he spent two years behind bars following his arrest in 2008 but also added: *"I regret it has not gone all the way, in a way I want my day in court for the truth to come out. We never had our say in court."*

He also expressed his sympathy with the Morgan family: *"I feel dreadful for Daniel's family, they have not seen any justice and I think they deserve that."*

In 2014, Rees, Fillery, and the Vian brothers launched a £4 million lawsuit against the Metropolitan Police Service. The action was brought on the grounds of false imprisonment, malicious prosecution, malicious falsehood, and misfeasance in a public office. Court papers claimed that besides there being a lack of evidence during the 2006 investigation, there was also *"serious misconduct in relation to creation and management of their evidence"* by the investigating team.

Rees also points out what he refers to as the "accepted narrative" that the original investigation in 1987 was hindered by police corruption. His argument is that it was not corruption at all, but rather incompetence on behalf of the original investigating team from Catford CID. This still may not reflect well on Rees's friend, Sid Fillery, but it is an argument borne out by the 1988 inquiry undertaken by the Hampshire Police Constabulary. Detective Chief Inspector Farley of Hampshire Police reported at the time that there was an *"obvious lack of direction, co-ordination, management and supervision"* and that the *"initial effort must be described as pathetic"*. But Farley concluded his report by stating that he had found no evidence of police corruption.

Following a written complaint by Rees, in which he outlined his grievances against the Met, in March 2014 the DPS launched an investigation into his claims called Operation Megan. A police spokesperson said: *"Following the receipt of a public complaint containing a number of allegations in relation to the MPS handling of the Daniel Morgan murder investigation an investigation was started by the Directorate of Professional Standards. That investigation is ongoing. There have been no arrests."*

When the case came to the High Court in January 2017, the barrister representing Rees and the Vians, Nicholas Bowen QC, argued that Detective Chief Superintendent Dave Cook's only concern was securing the convictions of his suspects and had a total disregard for the possibility of a miscarriage of justice. He said in court: *"The single-minded determination of the Met to pursue and convict them has blighted their lives for the last 29 years."* He claimed that all five investigations and the resultant 750,000 pages of documentary evidence had the sole purpose of incriminating Jonathan Rees, Glenn and Garry Vian, Sid Fillery, and Jimmy Cook, and that there was never any effort to pursue other lines of inquiry. Indeed, it is now thought that there were over forty possible suspects linked to Morgan's murder, many of whom were never properly investigated, a revelation that does support Rees's view that the Met were *"blinkered"* in their approach to the case.

Dave Cook's handling of Gary Eaton and James Ward was once more criticised. Bowen said that *"between 2005 and 2006, he* [DCS Cook] *coached and manipulated the two main witnesses, failed to investigate exculpatory lines of inquiry, suppressed documents, misled colleagues and lied to the trial judge."* With these damning indictments against him, Dave Cook removed himself to Scotland and refused to appear before the High Court.

Bowen went on to assert that without the *"concocted and obviously unreliable"* evidence provided by Eaton and Ward, there would have been no grounds to bring a prosecution against Rees and the other men. He concluded: *"It is our case that these claimants should not have been prosecuted at all in 2008 and that the prosecution was brought without reasonable cause and maliciously. They have been doggedly pursued for a murder that they have consistently protested was nothing to do with them and which should never have been the subject of yet further criminal process in 2008."*

On behalf of the MPS, Jeremy Johnson QC, accepted the criticism of Cook's handling of his witnesses but also pointed out that the case against Rees and the Vian brothers had not collapsed due to the dismissal of Eaton and Ward but because of issues surrounding the disclosure of evidence. He defended the Met's position, maintaining that *"there was a proper basis to arrest and prosecute each of the claimants....The evidence that was gathered by the police included multiple accounts from various of the claimants' associates to the effect that Mr Rees had wanted Mr Morgan dead, that he had paid his brothers-in-law, Glenn and Garry Vian, to carry out the murder, that Jimmy Cook was the getaway driver, and Sidney Fillery knew about the murder."*

Referring to Fillery's alleged role in the murder, Mr Johnson also told the court that there had been *"an insidious web of corrupt police officers active in South London in the 80s and 90s and some of those officers were suspected of involvement in Morgan's murder."*

In an article published in the *Croydon Advertiser* in November 2014 that championed the cause of Jonathan Rees, he continued to plead his innocence. He pointed to the lack of evidence against him, and to the Hampshire Police inquiry that found *"no evidence of police corruption."* He told the *Advertiser* then that *"they* [the police] *decided in the early days that I was involved in Daniel's murder and they became blinkered on that; they became obsessive about that."*

He spoke of the two years that he had endured in

custody following his arrest in 2008 while he awaited a trial that never came. He even denied involvement in the Kim James plot, despite their being alleged tape recordings of him conspiring with Simon James and Austin Warnes. He blamed a police informant, possibly a reference to Derek Haslam, for *"setting him up"*.

The article closes with Rees railing against his enemies in the Met: *"At the moment, I'm still angry and I still want blood. I want them gripping the rails. I want to see them suffer for what they did to me and my family."*

Jonathan Rees leaving the Old Bailey in2011 following the collapse of the case against him for the murder of Daniel Morgan (Photo: REX)

Until recently, Sid Fillery and his family were running a pub called the Lion Inn on the Norfolk Broads. However, some of the locals don't seem to be particularly enamoured with him. One of them posted on a local internet forum in 2016: *"It's such a lovely spot and yes reviews can be subjective but I've always thought of it as a dive and the landlord a grumpy old eccentric with no clue about customer service."* Of course, reviews can indeed be subjective and there are many to suggest that Mr Fillery has put his chequered past behind him and moved on to more agreeable pursuits.

7

Codename: Stakeknife

From 1981 to 1991 Ian Hurst worked in military intelligence for the British army. He spent much of his military career in Northern Ireland during the province's "dirty war" handling informants who had been planted deep within various paramilitary organisations such as the IRA and the UDA. As a member of the highly secretive Force Research Unit his role was to debrief British agents and to covertly pass information, false or otherwise, to terrorist organisations.

He was later to claim that up to half of all IRA members were actually in the pay of British intelligence. During a crackdown on collusion between the security forces and terrorist groups in the province, Hurst says that former Metropolitan Police Commissioner Lord Stevens told him that of 210 terrorist suspects who had been arrested only three were not found to be acting as agents for the British government.

The FRU's influence within Loyalist paramilitary groups was such that they could dictate their own targets, thereby eliminating, to some degree, the random killing of Catholic civilians and subversively encouraging the paramilitaries to focus on what the British army considered were more legitimate targets. One such target was believed to be Pat Finucane, a Belfast human rights lawyer with a reputation for successfully defending republicans. Finucane was shot 14 times by UFF volunteers as he ate Sunday lunch with his wife and three young children in February 1989. He died in front of his family. Allegedly it was British intelligence, and more specifically an FRU colleague of Hurst's, Brian Nelson, who had passed on Finucane's identity to those responsible for the killing.

The FRU's influence, however, was not restricted to Loyalist groups. Often referred to as their "crown jewel", and occupying a position at the very top of the IRA's high command, was a British double agent codenamed Stakeknife. Stakeknife was in charge of the IRA's internal security and his role was to hunt down and eliminate British agents within the organisation. It has long been suspected that the security forces in Northern Ireland frequently allowed the deaths of IRA targets including their own operatives and other FRU agents in order to maintain Stakeknife's cover such was his importance to them. Loyal IRA members were often falsely singled out as British agents and executed in order to protect genuine informants.

During a retrospective article on the subject published in the *Belfast Telegraph* in October 2015, Henry McDonald wrote: *"The main complaint made to the Police Ombudsman Dr Michael Maguire from the families of those Stakeknife and his IRA unit captured, interrogated, in some cases tortured and then killed is that in many instances these deaths could have been prevented. The families through their solicitors argue that instead the State chose to allow their loved ones to be killed in order to protect a valuable intelligence inside the PIRA, one which Sir General John Wilsey is reported to have said was the '... golden egg, something that was very important to the Army'"*.

The identity and location of Stakeknife was obviously highly sought after information. One of the few people to be in possession of such information was Ian Hurst. Stakeknife was of such value and his intelligence output so prolific that he had his own dedicated team of handlers within the FRU. He also had his own dedicated hotline with a contact number known only to him. Although Hurst was not one of his handlers, he stumbled across Stakeknife's true identity by chance one night whilst manning the phones. Journalist and close associate of Hurst's, Liam Clarke, subsequently wrote in the *Belfast Telegraph "Stakeknife had been caught drink-driving and gave uniformed police the hotline number in an effort to extricate himself."*

Following the IRA's 1987 Remembrance Day bombing in which ten civilians, many of them elderly, and one police officer were killed and a further 63 people injured, Hurst was posted to Enniskillen as part of the counter-terrorism operation in Fermanagh. Here he was to meet his future wife, a nurse called Noreen Sweeney. She was from a staunchly republican family from Donegal, something that Hurst later claimed to have changed his perspective on the "troubles". This republican connection of Hurst's was enough to adversely affect his security clearance within the intelligence service and in 1991 he took early retirement from the army.

Members of a British Intelligence FRU unit in Northern Ireland (Ian Hurst is circled)

It appears that Hurst's view of Northern Ireland's political landscape did somewhat alter during the 90s and by 1997 he was planning a book exposing the activities of British intelligence in the province. To this end, in 1999, Hurst and Irish journalist, Liam Clarke began to publish Hurst's accounts of his experiences in Northern Ireland in the *Sunday Times*. The articles were explosive and incredibly damaging to all those concerned. Hurst's tales of espionage, collusion, betrayal, and murder were the subject of condemnation and firm denial from both sides of the political divide. He was derided as a fantasist but, even so, became the subject of an injunction to prevent him from making any further revelations.

Under the pseudonym, Martin Ingram, Hurst finally published his book, *Stakeknife: Britain's Secret Agents in Ireland*, in February 2004. It was co-written by Belfast-based journalist Greg Harkin and published by The O'Brien Press in Dublin. As anticipated, Hurst revealed Stakeknife's identity as belonging to that of IRA veteran Freddie Scappaticci; an accusation that both the IRA and Scappaticci himself vehemently deny. For his part, Hurst quickly removed himself to the sanctuary of continental Europe.

But Hurst's story wasn't yet over. In 2011, it was once more dragged through the British media and the legitimacy of Hurst's claims again became the subject of debate.

In 2006, he had opened an email that he believed had originated from one of his contacts at the *Sunday Times* in London. It hadn't. In fact, it had been sent by a fellow former FRU operative called Philip Campbell Smith and contained in it a form of malware known as a Trojan horse. This would have given Smith complete control over Hurst's computer. He would have been able to access the hard drive, intercept private emails, and even spy on Hurst and his family via the computer's webcam.

But Smith wasn't acting independently. After retiring from the army he had set up as a private investigator and had been instructed to hack into Hurst's computer by none other than Jonathan Rees. Rees himself had been commissioned by the then editor of the *News of the* World's Irish edition, Alex Marunchak, to locate the whereabouts of Freddie Scappaticci. Given the ongoing injunction against Hurst and the sensitive nature of Scappaticci's whereabouts, it can only be assumed that this intrusion would have been considered a threat to national security.

Nick Davies takes up the story in *The Guardian: "The successful hacking of a computer belonging to the former British intelligence officer Ian Hurst was achieved in July 2006 by sending Hurst an email containing a Trojan programme which copied Hurst's emails and relayed them back to the hacker. This included messages he had exchanged with at least two agents who informed on the Provisional IRA — Freddie Scappaticci, codenamed Stakeknife; and a second informant known as Kevin Fulton. Both men were regarded as high-risk targets for assassination. Hurst was one of the very few people who knew their whereabouts."*

Despite the enormity of the security risk, despite the police and MI5 being aware of the hacking in 2007 and despite Smith being arrested in 2009 and his computers being seized by police, Hurst was not made aware of the intrusion until 2011 when reporter Stephen Scott from the BBC's *Panorama* programme tracked him down and showed him a copy of a fax that had been sent to Alex Marunchak on 5th July 2006 containing emails that Smith had stolen. Hurst immediately recognised them as having come from his own email account and suspected that his former FRU colleague was behind it. He told the BBC *"The hairs on the back of my head are up".*

He confronted Smith, a meeting at which he agreed to wear a hidden camera and microphone on behalf of the BBC; a meeting that was recorded and later broadcast. Smith admitted hacking Hurst's computer, and told him: *"It weren't that hard. I sent you an email that you opened, and that's it ... I sent it from a bogus address ... Now it's gone. It shouldn't even remain on the hard drive ... I think I programmed it to stay on for three months".* When Hurst asked Smith who had instructed him to hack his emails, Smith is heard on tape saying: *"The faxes would go to Dublin. He was the editor of the News of the World for Ireland. A Slovak-type name. I can't remember his f...ing name. Alex, his name is. Marunchak"*. Smith also claimed to have had regular contact with Andy Coulson during 2006, a period of time, during which Coulson was later to claim under oath that he had no knowledge of wrongdoing or of any criminal behaviour at the *News of the World*. When the BBC gave Marunchak the opportunity to respond to the allegations against him, he declined to speak to them.

Philip Campbell Smith

Because of these revelations by *Panorama* and because such criminal behaviour fell outside the remit of the Met's ongoing investigation into phone hacking, police were forced to launch a dedicated investigation into computer hacking called Operation Tuleta. This was to run alongside a separate investigation into the case of Ian Hurst. Matt Blake wrote in *The Independent* on 29th July 2011 that "*In the latest twist in the long-running phone-hacking scandal, the Metropolitan Police is assembling a new squad of detectives to look into claims that the News of the World stole secrets from the computer hard drives of public figures, journalists and intelligence officers.*"

A statement by the Metropolitan Police read: *"Since January 2011 the MPS has received a number of allegations regarding breach of privacy which fall outside the remit of Operation Weeting, including computer hacking. Some aspects of this operation will move forward to a formal investigation. There will be a new team reporting DAC Sue Akers."*

Scotland Yard also added: *"This started as an exercise to investigate the very serious allegations made by Panorama and enough evidence of criminality exists for there to be a successful prosecution. We understand that the hacking of computers by the NOTW covers a much wider period than the three months initially alleged by the BBC programme."*

At the beginning of October 2012 Rees and Marunchak were arrested by officers from Operation Kalmyk under Section 3 of the Computer Misuse Act 1990 and their homes were searched. Earlier in the year, Philip Campbell Smith had already been jailed for 8 months at Kinston Crown Court for separate offences involving the illegal gathering of personal information.

Rees was alleged to have received £4000 from the *News of the World* for commissioning research into the whereabouts of Freddie Scappaticci but, once more, charges against him were dropped due to a technicality. In September 2015 both he and Alex Marunchak were released from their bail conditions. Under the Computer Misuse Act, charges have to be brought no longer than three years after the alleged offence. As the hacking of Ian Hurst's computer had taken place in July 2006 and the police investigation that led to Rees and Marunchak's arrests was not launched until after the BBC's investigation in 2011, it was clear that they had run out of time to mount a successful prosecution. The Crown Prosecution Service released a statement that clarified their position regarding the case against Rees and Marunchak: *"Any decision by the CPS does not imply any finding concerning guilt or criminal conduct; the*

CPS makes decisions only according to the test set out in the Code for Crown Prosecutors and it is applied in all decisions on whether or not to prosecute."

Hurst was clearly disappointed and urged the CPS to review its decision not to prosecute. He proceeded with a civil action against News International, his lawyer, Mark Lewis, announcing that *"proceedings were lodged at High Court today against two News International companies and three individuals alleging the interception of emails and associated matters. Mr Hurst has made a complaint to the police that is being investigated."*

The failure of the Met to look further into the theft of his emails when it was first brought to their attention in 2007 and then their failure to bring a prosecution when they did finally launch an investigation led Hurst to believe that he had been the subject of a police cover-up. In fact, he told the London Evening Standard: *"My family and I were devastated to learn we had been targeted by the News of the World - and even more shocked to discover the Met knew about it four years ago and did nothing."* He added: *"Officers do not appear to have investigated these crimes which, given everything else that has happened, reinforces my belief that the Met is institutionally corrupt."*

Given the alleged involvement of Jonathan Rees, Alex Marunchak and the *News of the World*, Hurst began to join the dots and launched his own investigation into the connection between his case and that of Daniel Morgan. As part of his own personal inquiries, Hurst covertly recorded a telephone conversation with Derek Haslam, the former police officer and CIB3 informant who had worked undercover for Southern Investigations. This tape sheds more light on the activities of Jonathan Rees, what motivated him and the reluctance of the Met to take action against him.

Hurst: *"The point is that MPs, ministers, the Home Secretary, they were targets, and that information was communicated to your handlers."*

Haslam: *"And the reason is they fell into two camps of target, one that could be made, they could, er, financially make money from, and the other type was one that they could use, blackmail, or influence for their own benefit to do with their own thing, because they were so anti that squad."*

Hurst: *"So, yeah, you mean they see…"*

Haslam: *"Yeah, anything that could put the Met into a bad light, or anybody they could implicate, or blackmail into helping them, you know, in two. One would have been for earning money like Marunchak's end, and two would have been for influence."*

Hurst: *"But you can put your hand on your heart and you can say categorically that all intelligence which you generated which demonstrated a threat posed against an MP, a minister, or the Home Secretary was communicated to your handler?"*

Haslam: *"That's right."*

Ian Hurst later gave a statement to the Leveson Inquiry into media practices in which he was blunt in his appraisal: *"I am also absolutely certain that there were strong links between certain newspapers and former and current officers of the Metropolitan Police Service."* He also spoke of *"the unhealthy role of the police"* and asserted that *"if the hacking had been fully investigated by the police when it first came to light, further illegal information gathering would not have occurred."*

In a remarkable twist to the whole hacking saga, the IPCC announced in March 2017 that they were launching an investigation into Scotland Yard's alleged involvement in the illegal accessing of email accounts belonging to hundreds of peace campaigners and environmentalists along with what were seen by the Met as sympathetic politicians and journalists, including two unnamed members of *The Guardian* newspaper's staff.

The investigation centred on a letter anonymously sent to Greenpeace peer Jenny Jones, herself a former member of the Metropolitan Police Authority from 2002 until its abolishment in 2012. The letter was sent by a former member of the Met's National Domestic Extremism and Disorder Intelligence Unit (NDEDIU). The correspondent claimed that the Domestic Extremism Unit had used contacts in the Indian police force to hack into email accounts and obtain passwords which were then passed to officers at the secretive Scotland Yard unit.

In order to substantiate those claims, passwords belonging to ten of the accounts were also supplied. When lawyers acting on behalf of Baroness Jones were able to contact six of the alleged victims, they found that five of the passwords were an exact match and that the sixth was very close. One of the victims who was able to match his password with the one being illegally held by the Met spoke of feeling *"angry and violated"*. Another said: *"It's creepy to think of strangers reading my personal emails."*

The sender of the letter wrote that they had decided to expose these activities because *"over the years, the unit had evolved into an organisation that had little respect for the law, no regard for personal privacy, encouraged highly immoral activity and, I believe, is a disgrace."*

Another target of the unit was a man called John Catt, an octogenarian war veteran who became a peace campaigner shortly after the end of the Second World War. Mr Catt had no criminal record but liked to sit and sketch his friends at the various rallies they attended. In 2010 he took advantage of the Data Protection Act to find out what information the Met had on file about him. It was discovered that the Domestic Extremism Unit had a record containing 66 entries regarding his activities and that he had been under heavy surveillance since 2005. At the age of 91, Mr Catt was still pursuing his case through the European Court of Human Rights in an attempt to force the Met to delete their records of his non-violent and completely legal activities.

MP Tobias Elwood and members of the emergency services fight in vain to save the life of PC Keith Palmer following the 2017 terrorist attack in Westminster

The importance of the work of the Domestic Extremism Unit was brought into sharp focus only days after the IPCC announcement in March 2017 when a radicalised Islamic convert from Kent called Adrian Elms drove a rental car into pedestrians on Westminster Bridge, injuring scores and killing four before stabbing a police officer to death in the grounds of the Houses of Parliament. Unfortunately, and unlike John Catt, Elms (known as Khalid Masood) had apparently eluded the ever watchful eye of the unit. He was shot dead by police and fell only yards from PC Keith Palmer, the brave policeman whom he had so tragically murdered.

8

Theresa May, Nuala O'Loan and the Independent Panel

Current Prime Minister Theresa May was born in 1956 and rose to the highest possible position in British politics. Her father being a Church of England vicar, she grew up in a vicarage in Oxfordshire and always retained her Anglican faith. State educated, she later studied Geography at Oxford University before accepting a position at the Bank of England. Her real ambitions though lay in the field of politics and in 1997, during a period that had seen a downturn in Conservative Party fortunes generally, Mrs May swept into parliament as the new MP for Maidenhead. Although this was an election that saw a landslide victory for Tony Blair's New Labour, she had begun her ascent through the halls of Westminster.

When David Cameron resigned as Prime Minister following the European Union referendum in 2016, a referendum he called and then lost, plunging the Conservative Party into disarray, Mrs May became only Britain's second female Prime Minister following Margaret Thatcher. Tory grandee, Kenneth Clarke, likened May to "the Iron Lady", a former colleague of his, when he described the new Prime Minister as *"a bloody difficult woman"*. She became Prime Minister on 13th July and promised to provide the steadying hand that her party and the nation as a whole were in such dire need of. Her rise to power has been generally well-received, even *The Guardian* commenting that *"In a political party that struggles to shake off its elitist, old Etonian, yah-boo-sucks reputation, May represents a different kind of politician: a calm headmistress in a chamber full of over-excitable public schoolboys."*

Although Mrs May herself voted for the UK to remain as part of the European Union, it had befallen her to oversee the huge task of her country's withdrawal from the EU, insisting that there would be no second referendum and coining the phrase *"Brexit means Brexit".*

She raised her international profile still further when, on 27th January 2017, she became the first world leader to meet with controversial newly elected US President Donald Trump, a meeting for which she weathered much condemnation.

Prior to her residency at 10 Downing Street, Mrs May had served as Home Secretary from 2010 to 2016, making her the longest serving Home Secretary in the last 50 years, and only the second longest serving in a hundred years. She was a formidable Home Secretary, telling the Police Federation in a 2014 speech that corruption in the service was not only limited to *"a few bad apples".* She was determined to fight this corruption and it was during her stint at the Home Office that, on 10th May 2013, she announced that there would be an independent inquiry into the murder of Daniel Morgan and the police handling of the case. She told the House of Commons in a written statement that the inquiry would address questions relating to *"the role played by police corruption in protecting those responsible for the murder from being brought to justice and the failure to confront that corruption."*

The inquiry was to take the form of an Independent Panel along the same lines as the Hillsborough Inquiry into the death of 96 Liverpool football supporters in April 1989 and the police handling of that tragedy. The Hillsborough Inquiry had again highlighted the relationship between the police and the tabloid media. This time it was South Yorkshire Police and another News International title, the *News of the World's* sister paper, the *Sun,* who were the subject of public scrutiny. On Wednesday 19th April 1989, four days after the tragic events at Hillsborough Stadium in Sheffield, the *Sun* ran a story in which they pointed the finger of blame for the disaster at the fans themselves.

They reported how *"drunken Liverpool fans*

viciously attacked rescue workers as they tried to revive victims of the Hillsborough soccer disaster", "Police officers, firemen and ambulance crew were punched, kicked and urinated upon by a hooligan element in the crowd", "Some thugs rifled the pockets of injured fans as they were stretched out unconscious on the pitch".

The *Sun's* "malicious" reporting of the Hillsborough disaster

The *Sun* directly quoted one officer as saying: *"...we struggled in appalling conditions to save lives, fans standing further up the terrace were openly urinating on us and the bodies of the dead."* The *Sun* published the story under the banner headline *"The*

Truth" and claimed it to have come from high ranking sources within the South Yorkshire Constabulary. However, the inquiry found that it was far from the truth and that the police had fed false stories to the press in order to deflect responsibility for their own failings on the day. Kelvin MacKenzie, then editor of *The Sun,* was forced to issue an apology, but not until four years later when he was called to stand before a House of Commons Select Committee.

The Home Secretary appointed Sir Stanley Burnton to chair the Daniel Morgan inquiry. An experienced member of the judiciary, Sir Stanley was a former Lord Justice of the Court of Appeal. Shortly before his retirement in 2012, he had been criticised by Master of the Rolls, Lord Neuberger, during a speech he made at the University of Birmingham Student Law Society, for a lack of gravitas when appearing on the television cooking programme *MasterChef* during the course of which show Lord Justice Burnton said of one dessert that it was *"meant to be passion fruit and mango. I didn't detect the mango and there wasn't enough passion."*

Although Alastair Morgan and his family had campaigned tirelessly for nearly thirty years for a judicial review, with powers of prosecution, into his brother's murder and the subsequent alleged police cover-up, they were finally forced to accept that the Independent Panel, that had no such powers, was their only remaining route to the justice that they sought. Following the acquittal of Jonathan Rees and the Vian brothers in 2011, Alastair had said: *"This murder is only technically unsolved. The police have a very good idea who the killers were and five investigations have not resulted in a single conviction. The only way forward we can see now is a judicial inquiry."* He told the press: *"The ball is now firmly in Mrs May's court."*

Having been thwarted in their attempts over many years to seek a meeting with the Home Secretary in order to discuss the case, the Morgan's were finally granted an audience with Theresa May at the end of 2011. She offered the family the prospect of a Hillsborough-style inquiry and promised that they would be kept fully informed of events. Alastair said of that meeting: *"We had to decide whether to continue with the fight for a full-blown judicial inquiry backed by legal powers or take this opportunity. We had been going on for more than 25 years at this point. I thought let's go for it."*

He drew his own comparisons between his case and that of the Hillsborough disaster. *"There had been a judicial inquiry into Hillsborough but that only went so far. The Hillsborough panel was a far more successful operation. Frankly, we were just tired."* He also referred to what he described as *"a Murdoch/police distortion of the truth"* that had been exposed by the Hillsborough inquiry and likened it to the case of Daniel's murder: *"It's exactly the same, possibly worse."*

By May 2013, Alastair was forced to accept that there was very little possibility of a successful prosecution being brought against the perpetrators of his brother's murder, a sentiment that was echoed by Mrs May when she indicated that there was *"no likelihood of any successful prosecutions being brought in the foreseeable future."*

The family admitted that they were *"battle-weary"* and that the lengthy campaign for justice had been *"mental torture".* In welcoming Theresa May's announcement of the Independent Panel, Alastair commented that: *"We trust and hope that the panel will assist the authorities to confront and acknowledge this failure once and for all, so that we may be able to get on with our lives."*

Theresa May's hand may have been forced into conceding to some of the Morgan family's demands by circumstances surrounding another high-profile inquiry that was taking place at the time. The Leveson Inquiry into phone hacking had, in February 2012, heard evidence submitted by Jacqui Hames regarding the *News of the World's* intimidation of her and her family during the fourth investigation into Daniel Morgan's death that was being led by her then husband, Detective Chief Superintendent Dave Cook.

Hames's account of her experiences at the hands of the now defunct Sunday tabloid had far reaching repercussions. Former Deputy Leader of the Labour Party, Tom Watson, joined the clamour for a judicial review into the Morgan case. He expressed his horror that *"a journalist tried to undermine a murder investigation"* and publicly named Alex Marunchak as that journalist. He also insisted that *"Rupert Murdoch owes the Morgan family an apology. I also don't think he has made his last apology to the grieving parents of dead children."*

This reference to the *"parents of dead children"* referred to the parents of Milly Dowler, to whom Murdoch had apologised, and those of Holly Wells and Jessica Chapman, to whom he had not. Ten-year-olds, Holly and Jessica had been abducted and murdered in Soham, Cambridgeshire in August 2002. Shortly before their disappearance, they had been photographed wearing matching Manchester United shirts at a family barbecue. This picture was widely circulated to the media during the search for the girls.

In a speech he gave to MPs in 2012, Tom Watson claimed that the police possessed intelligence that Alex Marunchak had paid the relatives of Cambridgeshire police officers in return for information regarding the investigation into the two missing girls. He said: *"I believe the Metropolitan Police are sitting on an intelligence report from late 2002 that claims a police contact overheard Marunchak claim he was paying the relatives of police officers in Cambridgeshire for information about the Soham murders. These are allegations that as far as we know have not been investigated. I don't know whether these intelligence reports are accurate, but I do know Alex Marunchak was involved in writing stories about how the Manchester United shirts of those young girls were found."* At the time of Marunchak's article, details regarding the discovery of the girls' clothing had not been released to the press.

Watson also called for the circumstances surrounding Daniel Morgan's death to form part of the Leveson Inquiry because of the clear involvement in that case of staff from the *News of the World.* This was a suggestion that was resisted by Lord Leveson because of the innate complexity of the case, the vastness of the documentation involved, and the underlying danger that it may have derailed the Leveson Inquiry altogether.

In response to Tom Watson's outspoken support for his campaign for justice, Alastair Morgan had told *Socialist Worker* in 2012: *"We're delighted to have Tom Watson's support. We've also sent in a submission to the home secretary calling for a judicial inquiry and we're hoping to meet her fairly soon to discuss this."*

The Morgan inquiry itself was shortly to sail into troubled waters. As was the case in 2010 and 2011, the Met had difficulty in handling the estimated 750,000 documents relating to the case and by March 2014 only 700 documents had been handed over to the panel. The members of the panel were in disagreement over how to proceed in the face of the Met's lack of co-operation. Because the Independent Panel had no legal powers, they were unable to compel the MPS to disclose the evidence that they required, nor were they able to subpoena witnesses to give testimony. Cracks began to appear and, in November 2013, chairman Sir Stanley Burnton resigned his position, claiming that "personal reasons" were behind his decision.

Alastair Morgan said of the Met's inability or unwillingness to deliver on their promises that *"They have delayed and obstructed the panel."* He told the press that *"Our police were prepared to cover up the involvement of their own in a contract killing, which all the available evidence shows the victim was a whistleblower about police corruption."*

Tom Watson, his support for the Morgan case undiminished, went on record as saying *"It is extraordinary that a case involving police corruption has taken nearly two years to yield even a single document. Even for the Met it is a remarkable state of affairs. They are clearly refusing to cooperate with an inquiry that is in the public interest and has the authority of the Home Secretary."*

Prime Minister and former Home Secretary Theresa May

It took nine months for the Home Secretary to appoint Burnton's successor but when she did, she turned to a figure with an impressive track record for dealing with controversial issues involving the police. Baroness Nuala O'Loan, who accepted her new role in July 2014, was formerly Northern Ireland's first Police Ombudsman between 2000 and 2007, during which time she was responsible for exposing some of the British Intelligence community's darkest secrets during their years of collusion with paramilitary organisations in the province.

She had also been responsible for investigating the police handling of the August 1998 Omagh car bombing in which 29 people were murdered by the Real IRA, as well as two unborn babies, and 200 more injured and maimed. She found that MI5 and the RUC's Special Branch had received intelligence up to 11 days prior to the massacre that warned of the attack. A British mole inside the IRA was alleged to have told his handler that a huge bomb was being built. Another tip-off spoke of a significant terrorist attack taking place in the market town of Omagh. The date of the attack was even supplied: 15th August. Special Branch did nothing. There were no extra roadblocks put in place around the town in an attempt to apprehend the bomb car; a red Vauxhall Cavalier that later disappeared from the scene of the explosion before it could be properly forensically examined and tested for DNA. It was discovered some time later rusting and bereft of evidence in a police storage facility.

The security services' reluctance to act on the information they had received may have been prompted by a desire to protect their agents working undercover with the terrorist groups concerned. One of their intelligence sources was a British double-agent called Kevin Fulton, a former colleague of both Ian Hurst and Philip Campbell Smith from their FRU days. Fulton had crossed swords with O'Loan during her investigation into FRU collusion with Loyalist paramilitary groups. He said of her appointment to the Daniel Morgan Independent Panel *"Hannibal is at the gates. A lot of people need to be very afraid."*

Baroness O'Loan, herself, vowed *"to do everything in my power to ensure that the panel works effectively engaging fully with all the members of Mr Morgan's family, to produce a report which will shine a light on what happened to Mr Morgan, and how his case has been handled since 1987."*

Initially, the Panel's report into the Morgan case was expected within twelve months of the Home Secretary's announcement to the Commons in May 2013, but it was clearly understood from the outset that any overlap with the Leveson Inquiry or ongoing phone hacking trials would subject the publication of the Panel's report to delay until any related criminal proceedings were concluded. However,

Baroness O'Loan was quoted by Joanne Sweeney in the *Irish News* in January 2017, nearly four years after the Panel was set up, as saying *"We are in the writing-up phase; there's big bundles of documents to revisit, to rethink, as while there have been four investigations into the murder, there's been no answers."* She cast more doubt on the potential success of the inquiry when she explained to Ms Sweeney, *"We just go where the evidence takes us. If the evidence goes no further, then we can't either."*

A month after Nuala O'Loan's interview with the *Irish News*, an eye-catching headline in the *Guardian* read: *"Daniel Morgan murder: three men lose case against 'malicious' police".* Vikram Dodd's article announced that Mr Justice Mitting had ruled against Jonathan Rees and the Vian brothers in their civil action against the Met for malicious prosecution.

Acting on behalf of the claimants, Nicholas Bowen QC had told the court that *"The Met police attitude to this case from the beginning was blinkered, and a mindset developed which propelled the various investigations towards the goal of seeking the conviction of our clients irrespective of the fact there was no credible evidence against them."* Singling out Dave Cook, Bowen claimed that the now retired Detective Chief Superintendent *"became convinced and resentful that Rees and Southern Investigations had fixed up a surveillance operation of his own activities with the active cooperation of the News of the World"*

Although Mr Justice Mitting agreed that Cook's actions had *"amounted to the crime of doing an act tending and intended to pervert the course of justice"* he ruled that Cook's coaching of Gary Eaton, one of the key witnesses against Rees and the Vians, had been motivated not by a desire to procure false evidence but by a conviction that Eaton had been present at Daniel Morgan's murder but was too scared to tell the police what he had seen. In essence, Cook tried too hard to provide the evidence the prosecution demanded in order to deliver the convictions that he felt the case merited.

The High Court ruled that even without Eaton's tainted testimony, the Met had been in possession of enough evidence to justify bringing murder charges against Rees and Glenn and Garry Vian. However, in the case of Sid Fillery's charge of conspiracy to pervert the course of justice, the Met's case had relied solely on the discredited evidence of Gary Eaton. For this reason, Fillery won his claim of misfeasance in a public office against the Met and was awarded damages by the court.

Following the verdict, Alastair Morgan commented on behalf of "the only policeman he ever trusted": *"Whatever the conclusions of this judgment, we consider that it would be a travesty of justice if David Cook is allowed to become the scapegoat for the failures of the Metropolitan police over the decades in failing to confront the police corruption that lay at the heart of this case."*

In July 2018, Mr Justice Mitting's ruling was overturned by the Court of Appeal and Jonathan Rees along with Glenn and Garry Vian were awarded substantial damages against the Metropolitan Police Service for malicious prosecution. In her summing up, Lady Justice King, criticised Mitting's 2017 findings, telling the court: *"With respect to this very experienced judge, the outcome which he reached namely, that although acting corruptly DCS Cook was not also acting maliciously, may well appear to be counterintuitive to any ordinary member of the public."*

"To say that DCS Cook, a prosecutor guilty of perverting the course of justice by creating false evidence against the appellants was, on account of his belief in their guilt, not acting maliciously, is rather like saying that Robin Hood was not guilty of theft."

Former Metropolitan Police Assistant Commissioner John Yates who had overall command of the failed fifth investigation into Daniel Morgan's murder, later resigning from the Met following criticism of his handling of the phone hacking inquiry, wrote an article for the *Independent* in March 2013 in which he said of the Morgan case: *"It is one of the most, if not the most shameful episodes in Scotland Yard's history."*

Vast amounts of newsprint have been expended on the case but the question still remains: Who did kill Daniel Morgan? There have been five investigations that the public have been made aware of. The cost to the taxpayer is estimated from anywhere between £30 million to £100 million but still the Morgan family have not found the justice they have so enduringly sought for thirty years.

For his part, Alastair Morgan still harbours a great deal of frustration. Referring to the former *News of the World* in January 2015, he said *"They've been a poisonous influence on the criminal justice system for years."*

APPENDIX A

LIST OF SOURCES

Nick Davies *The Guardian*
BBC News
David Connett *The Independent*
Powerbase
Alex Hanton *Listverse*
Press Gang
Laurie Flynn & Michael Gillard *The Untouchables*
Peter Jukes *Byline*
Vikram Dodd *The Guardian*
Lisa O'Carroll *The Guardian*
Richard Pendlebury *Daily Mail*
Stephen Wright *Daily Mail*
Keiligh Baker *Daily Mail*
Wensley Clarkson *Daily Mail*
Joseph Curtis *Daily Mail*
Cahal Milmo *The Independent*
Mark Hughes *The Telegraph*
Martin Evans *The Telegraph*
Mark Townsend *The Observer*
Graeme McLagan *The Guardian*
Jason Deans *The Guardian*
John Plunkett *The Guardian*
Dominic Ponsford *Press Gazette*
murdermap.co.uk
Nicola Harley *The Telegraph*
Brittany Vonow *The Sun*
Tom Pettifog & Nick Sommerlad *Daily Mirror*
Mark Sweney *The Guardian*
Roy Greenslade *The Guardian*
Daniel Boffey *The Guardian*
Kim Sengupta *The Independent*
Paul Lashmar *The Independent*
Amelia Hill *The Guardian*
Jason Bennetto *The Independent*
Dan Sabbagh *The Guardian*
Jamie Doward *The Guardian*
Jon Swaine *The Telegraph*
Murray Wardrop *The Telegraph*
Jane Martinson *The Guardian*
Jenn Selby *The Independent*
James Cusick *The Independent*

Richard Wheatstone *Daily Mirror*
Bernard O'Mahoney *Wannabe in my Gang?: From the Krays to the Essex Boys*
Tony Thompson *The Guardian*
Keith Perry *The Guardian*
davecourtney.com
WalesOnline
Sandra Laville *The Guardian*
Claire Carter *The Telegraph*
Ian Gallagher *Mail on Sunday*
David Rose *The Independent*
Richard Edwards *The Telegraph*
James Sturcke *The Guardian*
Jenny Percival *The Guardian*
Helene Mulholland *The Guardian*
Mark Hughes *The Independent*
Haroon Siddique *The Guardian*
Channel 4 News
Rebecca Seales *Daily Mail*
London Evening Standard
Kirsty Whalley
Bromley Times
Croydon Advertiser
Martin Hickman *The Independent*
Liam Clarke *Belfast Telegraph*
Matt Blake *The Independent*
Socialist Worker
Gavin Stamp *BBC News*
The Economist
Martin Beckford *The Telegraph*
Eleanor Barlow *Liverpool Echo*
Owen Gibson *The Guardian*
Suzannah Hills *Daily Mail*
Tom Harper *The Independent*
BBC History
John Ware *BBC/The Telegraph*
Rosie Cowan *The Guardian*
Nick Hopkins *The Guardian*
Joanne Sweeney *The Irish News*
David Pallister *The Guardian*
Sarah Lyall *New York Times*
Kim Sengupta *The Independent*
Scott Lomax *Libertarian Alliance*
Mary Dejevsky *The Guardian*
Rob Evans *The Guardian*

APPENDIX B

The Leveson Inquiry
Witness Statement for Part 1 Module 2

WITNESS STATEMENT OF JACQUELINE HAMES

I, Jacqueline Elizabeth Hames, c/o Bindmans LLP, 275 Gray's Inn Road, London, WC1X 8QB will say as follows:

1. I make this statement in my capacity as a Core Participant to assist the Inquiry in relation to Part 1 Module 2 which deals with the relationship between the press and the police and the conduct of each. Where the contents of this statement are within my own knowledge they ate true and where the contents are not within my own knowledge I indicate the source of my belief and believe them to be true. I attach as Exhibit JH1 a bundle of relevant documents to which the page references in this statement refer.

2. I am a former Metropolitan Police officer and *Crimewatch* presenter. I joined the Metropolitan Police Service ('MPS') in 1977 at the age of 18 and became a Detective Constable, serving until January 2008 when I took early retirement. I am best known for my role as a presenter on BBC *Crimewatch* between 1990 and 2006 as a result of which I have first hand experience of the way in which the press and the police interact, gained from working on both sides, as follows:
(i) Working as a Detective specialising in major crime inquiries such as murder, rape and serial sex offences covering areas such as forensics, exhibits, interviewing witnesses and suspects, conducting enquiries, family liaison and various roles within incident rooms including that of Office Manager and, just prior to retirement, in the area of Organised Crime;
(ii)In 1987 I worked on the implementation team for the country's first Crimestoppers project based at New Scotland Yard, which launched in 1988. This was a partnership between the Metropolitan Police, private sector business and the media, and was the first of its kind. We forged good working relationships with newspapers and television channels to appeal on crimes and advertise the Crimestoppers helpline number.
(Crimestoppers is now a charity which people can call anonymously with information about crime);
(iii)In 1990 I became a regular presenter on *Crimewatch,* making appeals to the public live on BBC1 every month to help solve crime on behalf of the UK police service. This led to me contributing to many other factual television programmes, thus seeing the media from the inside. I also received some personal press attention and learnt lessons about how to deal with this sort of interest. Being in this unique position I walked a sometimes difficult path between the two. It was lonely at times as there was no one else to whom I could relate in the same position, and I received no support from the MPS Directorate of Public Affairs;.
(iv)In 2002/2003 during a career break, I worked as a part-time press relations officer for the National Crime and Operations Faculty, dealing with requests for information;
(v) Since leaving the police I have pursued my interest in women's safety issues, writing a book on personal safety with Fiona Bruce, undertaken security

consultancy within the private and charitable sectors and continue to deliver training in police/media relations and also more recently stalking. I have also continued working in the media on news and factual programmes and assisted with promotional safety campaigns across a wide range of media;

(vi)In 2006 I was asked to write and deliver a regular presentation to the Advanced CID course at the Metropolitan Police Crime Academy on Media Strategies within crime investigations;

(vii)Regrettably, I also have personal experience of being placed under surveillance by the *News of the World*, a deeply unpleasant experience which, I believe, arose from inappropriate relationships between crime suspects and that newspaper. I will say more of this below.

Increased openness

3. I will start with some general observations of how the press-police relationship has changed since I joined the force in the 1970s. The way that the police and the press interact has changed beyond all recognition. When I first joined it was a completely closed shop: all media enquiries were dealt with by what was then called the "Press Bureau" and only officers at the most senior level were authorised to speak to the media. In 1969 the MPS had been rocked when *The Times* exposed massive corruption within the CID and this led to strained relations between the press and the MPS, with stringent rules and heavy restrictions about officers talking to journalists.

4. The media followed this up with regular investigative exposure of corruption and alleged malpractice in programmes like *World In Action* and exclusive investigations by papers such as the *News of the World*. A defining moment came in the early 1980's when the BBC transmitted a series of 'fly on the wall' documentaries called *Police* following Thames Valley Police Officers. One episode featuring officers' demeaning treatment of a rape victim successfully changed the way police dealt with victims of sexual offences forever and was clearly a pivotal moment in how effective the media can be as watchdogs of the police. However, the constant barrage of criticism in the media did nothing to enhance officers' view of the motives of journalists and most tended to avoid contact at all costs. This view was further supported by the lack of positive press coverage of news stories involving the police.

5. This all changed when Sir John Stevens became Commissioner in 2000 and introduced the current "open door" policy by which officers are positively encouraged, sometimes even ordered, to allow the media access to operations and to explain all aspects of their work.

6. In the early days this created something of a 'free for all' for the press which jumped at the opportunity to have access to newsworthy and exciting incidents. Fly on the wall documentary teams appeared sometimes with little warning and officers had to deal with their presence, and journalists – both print and broadcast - would turn up on operations. For example I recall one occasion in around 2006 when the Intelligence Unit I was working on put together an operation for the Robbery Squad (the 'Flying Squad') to cover an armed raid on a warehouse at Heathrow Airport. It was suspected that a team of armed robbers were going to attempt to steal a large quantity of gold bullion. At the last minute Jeff Edwards the Chief Crime Reporter and a photographer from *The Mirror* were allowed to tag along thanks to their close association with one of the Flying

Squad supervisory officers. This resulted in a front-page story showing a picture of the robber sitting on the ground tied up, almost with a smile on his face, under a typically triumphant headline 'You're Nicked'. This is exhibited at page 1 of JH1. Whilst this was undeniably a good news story for the police, as the suspects had only just been arrested it was inappropriate and, quite aside from the contempt risk, lent an almost 'comic book' quality to serious criminal behavior. I am firmly in favour of openness but appropriate boundaries do need to be established. The gap between arrest and charge of a suspect is a very difficult area for the media who appreciate that, upon charge, the case becomes sealed by laws of sub-judice and their reporting will be severely restricted. Some, anxious to make the most of a good story, will rush out badly thought-out articles before this can happen.

7. The other aspect to this particular incident was that other newspapers and media outlets were upset that *The Mirror* had been given the exclusive rights which left many with the impression that favouritism and undue influence was being given to one publication.

8. The most recent version of the 'open door' policy in the MPS, dated June 2011, is at pages 2 to 7 of Exhibit JH1 and opens by saying (in the Introduction on page 4) that:

"This updated policy reflects the Met s continuing commitment to be open ...."

Among other things it states (on page 5 of JH1) that:

"...we seek to gain maximum positive media coverage..."

"It is our policy to be open and honest in dealing with the media... "

"We will tell the media things which:
  are in the public interest to know about
  help to show the public the way in which the police go about their work"

However it also sets out (page 6 of JH1) the importance of appropriate limits for the release of information:

"While advocating greater openness and contact with the media, this policy does not authorise any police officer or member of police staff to divulge information which is beyond their own area of personal responsibility or authority or which represents gossip or rumour. "

9. Whilst the Policy serves as a general outline, more detailed guidance is supplied in a document entitled: "MPS Media Relations SOP" (Standard Operation Procedures) which is exhibited at pages 8 to 23 of JH1. The guidance sets out that:
  In routine operational incidents and investigations:
Inspectors and above are authorised to speak to the media about their own areas of responsibility;
Officers below the rank of Inspector can speak to the media with the approval of a senior officer of Inspector rank or above (page 12 JH1).

In high profile cases such as serious crime, security, terrorism and major incidents:
There are special strategies for dealing with intense media interest including the appointment of a dedicated police spokesperson. In these cases *"it is unlikely that the GOLD commander or SIO would want other police officers or members of police staff to divulge information which goes beyond the agreed media strategy without his/her express permission"* (page 13 JH1).

10. This document also gives general guidance about "Withholding Information" and "Off the record" (page 14 JH1). Whilst the policy is wide ranging and helpful, I have found very few officers attending my courses who have heard of, let alone read, the document.

11. Whilst this increased openness is a positive development that I believe to be in the public interest, it has brought its own problems, especially for police officers who, with little or no training and/or limited experience of dealing with the media, have found themselves having to make difficult and stressful decisions in relation to the handling of information.

12. Prior to 2006, to my knowledge there was no media training available to most MPS officers. The Directorate of Public Affairs ran small presentation skills courses which were notoriously difficult to get a place on. Nowadays Trainee Detectives receive one hour on policy and media awareness from their course instructor, and later formulate and role-play a media appeal during a wider training scenario as part of their Detective Training Course. Newly promoted Detective Sergeants receive 1.5 hours of input on policy, authority levels and general media, plus conducting a media appeal. Detective Inspectors are given a half day during the Advanced CID Training Course. I present that input and have done so since 2006. The first two hours are spent covering subjects such as working with the media when investigating crime, negotiating the demands of 24 hour rolling news, how to conduct yourself during a media interview and the challenges and opportunities of new media and technology. We also explore issues created by the immediacy of modern news such as when the press may receive tip-offs from the public using mobile phones or Twitter and can be the first on the scene or indeed film events on their phones which can then sent on to news programmes to be broadcast almost immediately. Typically between 12 and 18 officers will attend the training and the content is often driven by the kind of questions that they ask. This is followed by three different practical role-play scenarios of broadcast interviews and appeals.

13. The Senior Investigators' Course for Detective Chief Inspectors ('DCI') and Detective Inspectors ('DI') dealing with the most serious cases involves two days training from an outside consultant with assistance from a working broadcast journalist and myself.

14. What is very clear from the sessions I present is that officers reaching the rank of DI do not generally feel well-equipped to handle the media and often find it stressful and difficult. Whilst they are keen to 'do the right thing' and supply appropriate information, they are also very worried about the media having some sort of hidden agenda and trying to catch them out. As such there is a lack of confidence and much suspicion. General frustration is often exhibited at the lack of guidance they are given and they feel ill-prepared.

149

15. Officers I have spoken to also sometimes feel aggrieved at the way some stories are covered in the print media. For example, an officer might spend a long time with a particular journalist to supply information about a story and trust is built up. However, because ultimately the decision about what is published rests with a news editor, once the journalist files the story to the news desk, the news editor may completely change the angle.

16. Another area that is constantly commented on is the closeness between some senior officers and publications or individual journalists. There is a common perception that there is a separate set of rules for some senior ranks when it comes to media relations. This may be because the very nature of a journalist's job dictates that they establish good relations with people in all walks of life who can provide accurate information and comment about events and it is particularly desirable to maintain this with someone clearly headed for higher ranks. Over the years these 'working' relationships can develop into genuine friendships that could further muddy the waters in terms of how they are perceived by others.

17. During my training presentation I pose the question: 'Do you think it is possible for police officers to have a good working relationship with a journalist whilst maintaining their professional integrity?'. Initially this would easily provoke a 90% to 10% response against with some very robust and extreme views being expressed. However, in recent years this has shifted and when I asked the question recently it was about 50/50. However in many officers, confidence in their own ability to deal with the media is still quite low and many still avoid having to do so wherever possible.

18. Whatever the particular issue, in my view MPS officers are inadequately prepared for the glare of the media spotlight that is now part of modern policing and find they are having to navigate complex media issues with very limited media training, Most of the delegates on my courses express the view that they would like this level of input earlier and indeed would like to spend longer on the subject. This need is particularly acute in the London area where the MPS has to meet the demands of the highly resourced 24-hour national news media and a media savvy population ready to act as unofficial journalists.

19. The first few hours after the discovery of a major crime are by their very nature chaotic. That is not to say they are not under control, but the flow of information can often be contradictory and pressure to release facts to the media can be immense.

20. It is in the nature of most investigations that some aspects have to be kept confidential, even from the family of victims. The circulation of misinformation can open up huge rifts of distrust between police and witnesses/victims.

21. Many journalists are often talented investigators and can find out information about a case almost in parallel with a police investigation. As police are restricted by compliance with the due process of criminal law, this can also lead to frustration on the journalists' part as they can be aware of significant developments, make their own judgements and feel that officers are being too secretive. Off-the-record briefings to established and well-known journalists are an effective way of managing the process and can help to build trust on both

sides. However in recent years the power wielded by the Crime Reporters Association has given the impression of a closed club of people given special treatment by the police.

22. Media relations within the MPS are supported by the Directorate of Public Affairs, a large civilian support department. There are 3 levels of operations, with the major desks covering individual departments such as:

(i) Press Bureau (24 hr press communications);
(ii) Corporate Communications (supporting the commissioner);
(iii) Specialist Operations, Diversity and media monitoring (all at New Scotland Yard).

Then there are four Area Press Offices and a Borough Press Liaison Officer (BPLO) at each Borough Police Station. The top two levels tend to recruit staff from either civil service communications departments or ex-journalists. The BPLOs tend to be entry level and as such generally have little or no press liaison experience, but are placed in a situation where they are advising officers who themselves have very little media training or experience.

23. There are a lot of very committed highly skilled press officers within DPA but the culture is set at the top and there has long been a sense of disquiet amongst many officers at the close nature of the relationship between people at the top of the Directorate of Public Affairs and print journalism. It may well be that as a result of all the negative press that I mentioned earlier, a genuine and honest effort was made to engage those in powerful media positions during the initial period of the new era of the 'open door' media policy, to try to tackle the reputational damage inflicted over the previous years. Whatever went on, the perception was that the Directorate of Public Affairs was more interested in serving the journalists and those at the top of the MPS than it was in the majority of police staff.

24. In my view the press-police relationship works well during high profile cases when an experienced officer is detailed to do nothing but handle media inquiries. This is what happened during Operation Sumac, the investigation sparked by the Ipswich serial murders in 2006. The investigation attracted enormous national and international coverage and a Detective Superintendent was nominated to handle the media, which he did very successfully. His previous experience and understanding of the case meant that he was well equipped to make appropriate judgment calls about what information could be released. At times there is an information vacuum where there is simply nothing that can be reported to the media. During those times someone dedicated can keep everyone interested for example, by providing background information about the victims, photographs, video or interviews with family or friends or general non-sensitive background information about the enquiry itself, thus preventing the media from filling the gap with mere speculation, but still maintaining the story's momentum with the public. As well as keeping the media happy and protecting the rights of those under investigation, this arrangement prevents the officers who are trying to conduct the actual investigation from being swamped by inquiries so that they can get on with their job.

25. In contrast to this, when a major incident breaks without a suitable media strategy being put in place, the situation can get completely out of hand very

quickly. The bottom line in many of these cases is that the press would love to be instrumental in solving the crime before the police do and, unless handled robustly, will try to 'run the show'. It is widely recognised that that is what happened during the first couple of weeks into the investigation that followed the disappearances of Holly Wells and Jessica Chapman from Soham in 2002. In the absence of an immediate robust police media strategy the media started to dictate police action. The press were putting pressure on the police to follow lines of investigation such as sightings called in by members of the public to the media, and criticised the police when they were not immediately followed up. Some examples of this are as follows:

Sunday August 2nd 2002: at approximately 10pm: Holly and Jessica were reported missing.

Thursday August 6th: *The Sun* offered a front-page reward of £150,000 without informing the police investigation team and *The Daily Express* offered a front page reward of £1m. *The Daily Express* did contact police on the eve of publication and were asked not to offer the reward without further discussion. *The Daily Express* went ahead and published the reward anyway. The effect of this was that the police received in the region of 12,000 calls from the public offering ideas, speculation and sightings of the girls at locations all over the country, thereby swamping the incident room. In addition people began arriving in Soham from far and wide to search the streets and surrounding countryside.

Tuesday August 11th: *The Daily Mirror* reported on a sighting of a "green car" containing two children on the back seat heading towards Newmarket Racecourse.

Wednesday August 12th: *The Daily Express* reported that a "jogger" believed he may have heard screams at Newmarket racecourse the night the girls disappeared. The effect of this was that Police spent all night excavating part of Newmarket racecourse and discovered nothing.

Thursday August 13th: *The Sun* headline that day was: "Not one clue" and *The Daily Mail* headline: "Back to Square One". This was extremely demoralising for the investigating officers who were in fact following up many lines of enquiry.

26. The media consultant called in to assist Operation Sumac was Matt Tapp of Matt Tapp Associates who is also currently Head of Communications at Nottinghamshire Police. Mr Tapp has conducted research into rewards offered by newspapers to the public for information in solving crime between 1992 and 2002 and discovered that, during that period, rewards in excess of £2 million had been offered by British newspapers from the News International stable alone and no money had been paid out.

27. On Day 10 of the Soham investigation Mr Tapp was brought in by the police and took control of the police media strategy ensuring that the media were kept up to date with developments but also that, when there were none, suitable material was supplied to keep the press focussed on the relevant official appeal points.

28. Turning to another example, I recall working on a murder case in a tower block in Feltham in the mid 1990's in which an elderly couple had been murdered and mutilated. The police were called at about 2 am and by the time we got there and set up an incident room the press had already knocked on the doors of the tenants of the tower block and learnt about the mutilation angle. At that point we had not informed the victims' family about the mutilation and,

because we were told that the press were on their way to see the family, we had to rush round and inform them of this aspect of the crime when we would like to have handled things differently. We also had a fly on the wall documentary team working alongside us who, when the suspect was arrested, were instructed not to take footage of him in police custody. It turned out that they had used a hidden camera and in fact transmitted his image against the wishes of the Investigating Officer. Whilst the PCC Code is designed to prevent certain behaviour, such as intrusion into grief or shock, in my experience, if there is a good enough story, the press will tend to disregard the Code.

My personal experience of media surveillance

29. As well as encountering press-police issues during my professional life, I have also unfortunately had first-hand experience of being placed under surveillance by the *News of the World*.

30. In 1987 a man called Daniel Morgan was murdered and found dead in the car park of the Golden Lion Pub in Sydenham, South London. He had been hit in the head with an axe. Mr Morgan was a private investigator with the company 'Southern Investigations', which he ran with his business partner, Jonathan Rees.

31. The initial murder investigation was compromised when it was discovered that Metropolitan Police officers had been corruptly involved with Southern Investigations and that Rees, a suspect, was also a friend of Detective Sergeant Sid Fillery, a member of the murder enquiry team. After that enquiry was completed, Fillery medically retired from the Police and became Rees' business partner at Southern Investigations. No one was charged in connection with Mr Morgan's murder.

32. In 1988 Hampshire Constabulary conducted an enquiry for the Police Complaints Authority (PCA) after a complaint was lodged by Mr Morgan's family. Whilst Hampshire police concluded that they had sufficient evidence to charge Rees with Mr Morgan's murder, the DPP considered the evidence and discontinued the case.

33. In 1997 the Metropolitan Police's Directorate of Professional Standards (DPS) initiated a further investigation using covert evidence gathering techniques concentrating on the business premises of Southern Investigations, from where Rees and Fillery still operated. This investigation was thwarted when Rees and others (including a serving police officer) were identified as having planted cocaine on a woman to assist her husband, (their client), to get custody of their son. To prevent a miscarriage of justice, those implicated were arrested and Rees was convicted and sentenced to seven years imprisonment. Fillery continued running Southern Investigations in his absence.

34. In 2002 the police decided to issue a fresh appeal for information in connection with Mr Morgan's murder. My then husband, David Cook, who was then a Detective Chief Superintendent, was tasked with being the public face of the inquiry by appearing on *Crimewatch*. He duly made the appeal on 26 June 2002, asking for anyone with information to come forward and announcing a £50,000 reward. He later became the Senior Investigating Officer (SIO) on the inquiry, which lasted until March 2011. After the appeal was transmitted, the

MPS received intelligence that one of the suspects in Southern Investigations had been discussing David's involvement in the inquiry and intended to make life difficult for him. A police panic alarm was installed in our house, along with additional security and we were placed under the umbrella of the Witness Protection Unit.

35. During this period an email was received at the *Crimewatch* production office suggesting that I was having an affair with a Senior Police Detective. Whilst completely untrue, this obviously caused me some considerable concern, as it was clear someone was trying to stir up trouble for me at the BBC and damage my reputation. I also remember that someone had rung Surrey Police Finance Department pretending to be from the Inland Revenue and attempting to obtain our home address. This was identified quickly as bogus and no information was given out. We also identified one occasion when our mail had been tampered with.

36. David decided to start going into work later, walking our dog and taking the children to school. One morning around the 10th July 2002 he saw a van parked in the park opposite where we lived, which aroused his suspicions. The following day there were two vans. When he left later to take my son and daughter to nursery and school, both vehicles started following him and it was clear he was being kept under surveillance.

37. When it happened again, (which may have been the following day although I am not now sure), he was able to contact other police officers who arranged to have one of the vehicles stopped because of a broken tail light, He later told me that the vehicles were leased to News International and that Southern Investigations had close links to the *News of the World* through the senior news editor Alex Maranchak. I also spotted a white van in the lane opposite my house. There were two occupants who I believed were taking photographs. I passed the details to our witness protection officers and left the house by the back entrance.

38. This series of incidents caused us great anxiety. Our house was on the market for sale at the time and with the worry over allowing strangers access to our home, it had to be taken off, causing us to review our plans to move house. We had to speak to the headmistress of my daughter's school and the head of my son's nursery to highlight the possibility of strangers hanging around outside. These were not easy conversations in light of concerns generally about child safety. We also had to consider carefully whether inviting our children's friends round to the house was sensible. In fact all aspects of our daily lives had to be reconsidered in light of these events.

39. Dick Fedorcio, the Head of the MPS Directorate of Public Affairs, duly sought an explanation from Rebekah Brooks (then Wade) who was then editor of the *News of the World*. The explanation supplied by the *News of the World* for placing David and I under surveillance was that they were investigating suspicions that we were having an affair with each other. This was utterly nonsensical as we had by then been married for four years, had been together for 11 years and had two children. Our marriage was common knowledge to the extent that we had even appeared together in *Hello!* magazine.

40. The *News of the World* has never supplied a coherent explanation for why we were placed under surveillance. In 2003, David, together with Dick Fedorcio and Commander Andre Baker, met Rebekah Brooks to discuss the matter. She repeated the unconvincing explanation that the *News of the World* believed we were having an affair. She agreed to look into Alex Marunchak's associations with Rees and Fillery but to my knowledge nothing further was ever said about the subject, indeed Mr Marunchak was subsequently promoted. I believe that the real reason for the *News of the World* placing us under surveillance was that suspects in the Daniel Morgan murder inquiry were using their association with a powerful and well-resourced newspaper to try to intimidate us and so attempt to subvert the investigation. These events left me distressed, anxious and needing counselling and contributed to the break-down of my marriage to David in 2010. Given the impact of these events, I would like to know why the police did not investigate why we came to be placed under surveillance by a newspaper like this.

41. In May 2011 police officers from Operation Weeting contacted me and informed me that my details had been found in Glenn Mulcaire's notebooks. I was then shown details of investigations undertaken by the *News of the World* into David and I back in 2002, which I had had no idea were going on at the time. The information that I was shown in the notebooks included detail such as my payroll and warrant numbers, the name of the police section house that I lived in when I first joined the police in 1977, the name, location and telephone number of my place of work in 2002, my and David's full home address and mobile phone number and some notes about my previous husband and his work details. The notes also contained notes about David, including his name, telephone number, rank and reference to "appeal" which I presume to be a reference to his appeal for information on *Crimewatch.* The date at the top of the notes was 3 July 2002, a week or so before the *News of the World* vans began to appear outside our home. This demonstrates to me that the *News of the World* knew full well that I was married to David at the time of the surveillance and thus gives the lie to their explanation for it.

42. This information could only have come from one place: my MPS file. I was horrified by the realisation that someone within the MPS had supplied information from my personnel file to Mr Mulcaire, and probably for money. Similarly distressing was the realisation that the MPS had known about these entries in Mr Mulcaire's notebooks since 2006 but had chosen neither to inform me nor to investigate it adequately. Normal procedure when faced with a large quantity of documentary evidence during an enquiry would be at the very least to analyse samples of it to ascertain its significance and scope the benefits of further investigation time being spent. This was particularly worrying because at the time when the information must have been leaked I was serving in a covert intelligence unit on a highly sensitive inquiry concerning airport security. If I had been given any indication that my mobile number had been compromised I would have changed it immediately to avoid any potential security breaches. I have always been loyal to the MPS but I do feel very let down by this failure to inform or protect me from the unlawful actions of the press.

43. It is the media's job to set the agenda for public concern, a position of huge responsibility easily open to abuse if left unchecked, particularly when balanced against the economic demands of supporting a profitable business. Whilst there

are guidelines in place for the press, it is the lack of transparency in the basic decision making process when it comes to whether and how a story is pursued, which in my view has caused the problems. I have heard stories from journalists about how they paid police officers for information and have then criticised the police service for corruption. I find this deeply hypocritical. Instead of paying these officers, they should have been exposing corruption within the police. That is not to say I disapprove of genuine whistle-blowers. There has to be a place of last resort at times of genuine desperation when there is nowhere else to go. But if exceptions are to be made, proper enquiries have to be made to ensure this goodwill is not abused.

44. When police investigators make decisions as to whether to undertake covert action against individuals, it has to be justified and the action taken has to be proportionate to the nature and seriousness of the allegation. Consideration is also given as to the potential impact on the subject, and anyone else who could be caught up in the action taken. That decision-making process is recorded and therefore open to scrutiny should problems or counter allegations arise at a later stage. I do not see why this should not also apply to journalists employing these tactics and the use of private investigators to delve into the privacy of individuals as well.

45. Looking forward in terms of how to ensure this situation never arises again, I do not believe that it is necessarily the answer to bring in more legislation when there is much already in place. It is more the case that nothing was implemented or adhered to. For instance, Section 2 of the Protection from Harassment Act 1997 gives police powers to act when an individual is subjected to two or more incidents of harassment causing them 'alarm or distress'. The Act also provides a civil remedy for individuals under Section 3 if victims prefer not to go down the criminal law route. This is simple and powerful legislation that is under-used and provides a route for redress should an individual wish to pursue it.

46. The police service needs to be seen as being totally independent and therefore fair and even-handed in its implementation of the law and brave enough to take a stand against media wrongdoing, even if it means the police could be subject to attack and criticism as a result. No one joins the police to be popular but a reputation of fairness and honesty is paramount. Good relations and partnerships with the media are very important, but the price in recent years has been too high. The public needs to be reassured as to the police's role as a beacon of safety and discretion. Reporting crime as a victim or witness can often be one of the most difficult and vulnerable times of someone's life, and a time when trust in the police is a crucial part in how the person copes with it. In recent years that respect has been tainted and I sincerely hope that this Inquiry acts as a crossroads and the police take this opportunity to improve their relationship with the public and to re-establish the trust that it so badly needs to be effective.

47. With regard to the press, for me the issue is about transparency and proportionality. I, (and I believe other members of the public), do not want to curb the media in exposing wrongdoing and hypocrisy, but every institution has to be seen to abide by rules of professional and ethical standards. However good the majority of police and journalists are, the public's faith in both has been damaged and we need reassurance that, should the mark be overstepped in the future, there will be severe consequences.

48. Recommendations

A clear complaints procedure for police officers wishing to correct inaccuracies in a story or who are unhappy with the conduct of a journalist;

Enhanced training in media and communication skills for officers at all levels of the police service;

Review of the role of the Crime Reporters Association to ensure transparency in terms of access to information;

News editors should be required to complete decision logs where invasion of an individual's privacy and/or use of a private investigator is contemplated.

APPENDIX C

Home Affairs Committee Supplementary written evidence submitted by Commander Peter Spindler, Directorate of Professional Standards, Metropolitan Police.

I write in response to your letter dated 29 May 2012 and want to thank you for the opportunity to clarify my answers to the Committee on 7 February 2012. I think it is important for me to contextualise the questions and answers I gave in response.

Firstly, at Q113 you began by stating that you "had received written evidence that police officers have accepted payments for information...." I was then asked whether I had seen evidence of police officers receiving payments for information. My reference to "evidence" needs to be seen in the context of the qualification at Q116. It is there that I confirm we have "intelligence" about corrupt activities however getting it to a stage of proof, where in police parlance it is to an "evidential standard" is a different matter.

I was unaware of what the "written evidence" you were referring to at the time and therefore unable to answer your question case specifically. However, even if I had known the specifics, it would have been inappropriate for me to comment further than I knew of allegations at the time, due to the sensitive nature of any ongoing counter corruption investigation.

I have since asked for a recall of historic cases known to the Directorate of Professional Standards Intelligence Bureau and have identified three which relate specifically to private investigation companies and therefore may be of interest to the Committee. I have attached a précis of these and will be more than happy to discuss them in greater detail when we meet with DAC Gallan at New Scotland Yard on 7 June to discuss the broader corruption profile.

APPENDIX TO LETTER TO KEITH VAZ MP

Operation Barbatus

Six men were sentenced in connection with what was one of the most extensive investigations ever carried out by the Metropolitan Police Service (MPS) anti-corruption team. The offences were committed between 1999 and 2004 and were identified by a pro-active, intelligence-led operation. The offences included conspiracy to cause unauthorised modification of computer material, conspiracy to defraud, conspiracy to intercept communications unlawfully, conspiracy to cause criminal damage to property, and aiding and abetting misconduct in a public office.

Those convicted included two former MPS constables, Jeremy Young and Scott Gelsthorpe, who had established a private investigations company, Active Investigation Services (AIS), three other ex police officers, two of whom were working as private investigators, and one further man also employed as a private investigator.

AIS used sophisticated bugging and IT technology to hack into computers and tap landline telephones engage in corporate espionage and invaded the privacy of members of the public. Among the illegal services offered by the company were accessing medical records, bank details and phone bills as well as fitting bugs to people's cars.

The investigation found that the men were illegally obtaining information from the PNC, including checks on people and vehicles. An audit of the details requested found they had all been checked by one of the men, who at the time was an Acting Inspector in Staffordshire Police.

Operation Two Bridges

This was an investigation into Law and Commercial (previously Southern Investigations) and brought to light evidence re the planting of drugs on the wife of Simon James (a client) to ensure he won a custody battle for the couples son. Ultimately James (seven years) Jonathan REES the PI (seven years) and Austin WARNES, serving MPS officer, (five years) were imprisoned for Conspiracy to Pervert the Course of Justice.

Operation Abelard

The investigation into the murder of Daniel Morgan instigated after a review of the murder by the MPS Murder Review Group; no charges resulted from this first Abelard investigation. Operation Abelard II brought together material from the previous investigations and as a result, William Jonathan Rees, was amongst four men charged with murder. Mr Morgan had worked with Mr Rees in Southern Investigations. This prosecution failed in March 2011 owing to disclosure issues (the prosecution offering no evidence). A fifth man, serving MPS police officer Sidney Fillery, had also been charged with perverting the course of justice, it being alleged he had interfered with the investigation (this charge was stayed in February 2010). Fillery subsequently retired and became Rees' partner in Southern Investigations. The corruption allegations surrounding the initial investigation led to the then PCA appointing Hampshire Police to investigate, however their report did not identify any corruption.

June 2012

APPENDIX D

Transcript of speech made by Labour MP Tom Watson to Parliament, 29th February 2012

Mr Tom Watson (West Bromwich East) (Lab): It is nearly 25 years—10 March 1987—since the son of Isabel and the brother of Alastair, Daniel Morgan, was brutally killed by five blows of an axe to the head. The last blow was probably struck when he was on the ground, because the hilt was embedded in his skull. Alastair is here today representing his family to hear the Minister's response to the family's call for a judge-led inquiry into the five failed investigations into Daniel's murder. All they ask is justice for Daniel.

The five failed inquiries have cost the taxpayer nearly £30 million. I believe that had the murder been investigated adequately a quarter of a century ago, Daniel's killer would have been brought to justice. John Yates said:

"This case is one of the most deplorable episodes in the entire history of the Metropolitan Police Service."

He went on to say that Daniel's family had "been treated disgracefully." I suspect that the Minister will not be able to grant a judge-led inquiry today, but I hope that he will at least keep an open mind, as the Home Secretary has not yet decided whether to grant such an inquiry, which my hon. Friend the Member for Islington South and Finsbury (Emily Thornberry) has also been campaigning for on behalf of her constituents.

I ask the Minister for one thing: please agree to ask his officials and the Metropolitan police a number of searching questions before he and the Home Secretary make their decision. I will put those questions to him at the end of my contribution. Daniel's family categorically do not want another investigation by the Metropolitan police—they have lost trust. Before I raise specific questions for the Minister, I will run through the events that have led to the five failed investigations.

Investigation No. 1 was severely compromised by police corruption. For 20 years the Met failed to admit that, despite the repeated pleas of the Morgan family. Indeed, it was not until 2005 that the Met's then commissioner, Sir Ian Blair, admitted that the first inquiry involving Detective Superintendent Sidney Fillery had been compromised. If that admission had come earlier, the subsequent inquiries might not also have failed.

As part of the first investigation, it is now known that DS Sid Fillery—a member of the original murder squad—failed to reveal to his superiors that he had very close links with Jonathan Rees when he became part of the inquiry. I am told that Fillery took a statement from Rees, but it did not include details that both he and Rees had met Daniel at the Golden Lion pub the night before the murder, nor did it include details of a robbery of Belmont Car Auctions a year earlier. Had those details emerged at the time, they would have revealed that those incidents brought both men into direct conflict with Daniel.

The Belmont Car Auctions story was significant because Jonathan Rees and Daniel had previously agreed that they would not deal with cash-in-transit work. Daniel is known to have been angry when Jonathan Rees took on the job of looking after the takings from the auctions, saying it would, "backfire on them." Rees, who was contracted to carry cash to the bank after a series of auctions, alleged that the bank night-safe had been interfered with, and therefore took the money to his home in March 1986. He alleges that he was attacked outside his house by two masked men who took the £18,000 from him. Belmont Car Auctions then sued Southern Investigations, which resulted in Daniel having to raise £10,000 very quickly for security to the court.

We know that two days before the murder Daniel told a witness, Brian Crush, that he believed that Rees and Fillery had set up the robbery and taken the money themselves. Daniel also told a witness that he was dealing with police corruption and that he did not know whom in the Met he could trust with the information.

It is important that the Minister understands at the outset why the omissions of the meeting at the Golden Lion pub and the auction robbery were so critical to the first investigation being compromised. My source has told me that omissions in the statement gathered by Fillery initially prevented attention being drawn towards Jonathan Rees and, indeed, Fillery himself. Alastair Morgan, Daniel's brother, has also told me how he raised his own suspicions with Fillery about Rees's possible involvement with the Belmont Car Auctions robbery as a possible motive for the murder. Alastair had not known that Fillery had actually recommended Rees to the auction company at the time.

Alastair now believes that it was a mistake to trust Fillery. He tells me that, for example, his information to Fillery later led to a phone call to his sister-in-law in which the family were told directly by Fillery that Alastair should get out of London because he was interfering in the investigation. When Fillery was removed from the team, the investigation quickly focused on those whom the Met believed to be responsible. Fillery, Rees, the two Vian brothers and two other police officers who were closely associated with Southern Investigations were arrested. However, no charges were brought and all six men were released.

At the inquest in April 1998, Kevin Lennon, who worked as a bookkeeper at Southern Investigations, gave evidence that implicated Rees in Daniel's murder. *The Guardian* newspaper reported that, in evidence to the hearing, Kevin Lennon said Rees wanted Morgan dead after a row. Lennon said:

"John Rees explained that, when or after Daniel Morgan had been killed, he would be replaced by a friend of his who was a serving policeman, Detective Sergeant Sid Fillery."

Lennon also told the inquest that Rees had said to him:

"I've got the perfect solution for Daniel's murder. My mates at Catford nick are going to arrange it."

Lennon added:

"He (Rees) went on to explain to me that if they didn't do it themselves the police would arrange for some person over whom they had some criminal charge pending to carry out Daniel's murder".

In the weeks before his murder, Daniel Morgan had repeatedly expressed concerns over corrupt police officers in south London. The Morgan family also believe that Daniel was about to reveal evidence of corruption.

In the aftermath of the murder and just as predicted by the evidence of Kevin Lennon seven months before at the inquest in 1988, Fillery took early retirement with an enhanced sick pension. Alastair Morgan has also told me how, at the inquest, members of the Met disputed the fact he had ever spoken with Fillery directly as part of the investigation. He believes that they were trying to cover up for Fillery.

Investigation No. 2—an outside inquiry—ordered by the then commissioner, Sir Peter Imbert, following a complaint by the family, was carried out by Hampshire police. It made no attempt whatsoever to address the allegations that Fillery had tried to get Daniel's brother, Alastair, out of London after he had pointed to Rees as a prime suspect in the murder. Had the inquiry done so, it might have found that what Alastair said tallied with the allegations previously made by Kevin Lennon at the inquest in 1988. The inquiry's terms of reference were to investigate

"all aspects of police involvement arising from the death of Daniel Morgan".

Unknown to Daniel's family, the remit of the inquiry was secretly changed at a high-level meeting at Scotland Yard in December 1988. The family further believe that the second investigation did not address the statements made at the inquest by serving police officers in which they denied that Alastair Morgan had ever raised his suspicions about Rees with Fillery, directly, as part of investigation No. 1.

In addition, Mr Morgan is frustrated that he offered to provide Hampshire police with a statement after an initial interview, but they refused it—indeed, no further statement was taken until 2000. The inquiry later reported to the Police Complaints Authority that there was

"no evidence whatsoever of police involvement in the murder" and that the original inquiry had been good.

Understandably, the Morgan family kept up their campaign for justice. In November 1997, they met Sir Paul Condon who promised to review the case—nothing happened until late 1998 when, under the leadership of John Stevens and

Roy Clark, the Met launched a third investigation into the murder. That was done without the knowledge of the Morgan family and in secrecy—not including the family was a mistake and the secrecy of the inquiry has deeply troubled them. The secrecy today is still a major issue for the family with the Met. I hope that the Minister understands that he must ask why the family were not kept informed.

As part of investigation No. 3, a covert bug was placed in the office of Southern Investigations. I will return to that later. Yet investigation No. 3 arguably missed its chance to use trigger events to gather further evidence on the murder. After Rees went to jail, the Morgan family had another meeting with Roy Clark. Clark initially said that they would do another investigation. The family ruled that out, as they wanted disclosure of the Hampshire report first. First Clark and then Andy Hayman refused to disclose the report to the family. It was not until the family were forced to go to the High Court that they succeeded. The Morgans should not have had to do that.

In the interim, the Met conducted a fourth inquiry, led by Detective Chief Superintendent David Cook. However, the fourth investigation, which the family described as the first honest investigation into the murder, gathered insufficient evidence to prosecute Rees, Fillery and three other men for the murder. My right hon. Friend the Member for Salford and Eccles (Hazel Blears) then refused the family's request for a judicial inquiry.

In 2006, a fifth investigation began under Assistant Commissioner John Yates. That happened out of the blue after Alastair Morgan had initially approached the Metropolitan Police Authority chairman, Len Duvall. He had ordered the commissioner to present his own report on the case before that. The family were initially deeply sceptical of the new Yates investigation. Devastatingly, after five years, the case collapsed last year. The Morgan family's solicitors have said that this was

"under the weight of previous corruption".

The accused, Jonathan Rees, Fillery and the Vian brothers were ultimately acquitted because the defence would not have had access to all the documents in the case. The Metropolitan police repeatedly mislaid crates of evidence, owing to the sheer number of documents the case had generated. Mr Justice Maddison also ruled that the supergrass witnesses had been mishandled.

I now turn to the situation that the family find themselves in now. Since the collapse of the prosecution, the Met has publicly admitted corruption in the first inquiry. The family believe this corruption had an impact on the second, third, fourth and fifth inquiries. However, what the family did not know during any of the five investigations is the extent to which the relationship between News International, private investigators and the police had an impact on the conduct of the inquiry.

Jonathan Rees and Sid Fillery were at the corrupt nexus of private investigators, police officers and journalists at *News of the World*. Through the hacking scandal, we now know that Southern Investigations became the hub of a web of police and media contacts involving the illegal theft and disclosure of information obtained through Rees and Fillery's corrupted contacts. Southern Investigations sold information to many newspapers during the 1990s, but we think exclusively to News International after Rees was released from jail in 2005.

The main conduit at News International was Alex Marunchak, chief crime reporter for the *News of the World* and later the paper's Irish editor. I want to focus the Minister's attention on Marunchak in particular. Rees and Marunchak had a relationship that was so close that they both registered companies at the same address in Thornton Heath. Abbeycover, established by Rees and his colleague from News International, Greg Miskiw, was registered at the same address as Southern Investigations, run by Rees and Fillery. Rees's confirmed links with Marunchak take the murder of Daniel Morgan to a new level.

It is important to remember that, in the days before the murder, Daniel's family believe that he was on the verge of exposing huge police corruption. That was confirmed by Brian Madagan, Daniel's former employer, in a statement in May 1987, in which he said that he believed Daniel was about to sell a story to a newspaper. In a second, later statement, Madagan said he believed that paper to be the *News of the World* and the contact to be Alex Marunchak who, until recently, still worked for the paper. BBC Radio 4's "Report" programme also confirmed that it has seen evidence suggesting that, a week before the murder, Daniel was about to take a story exposing police corruption to Mr Marunchak and was promised a payment of £40,000. We also know, from the investigative reporting of Nick Davies at *The Guardian*, that Southern Investigations paid the debts of Alex Marunchak.

As part of the third failed investigation, Operation Nigeria was launched. It included the surveillance of Southern Investigations between May and September 1999 and was run by the Metropolitan police's anti-corruption squad, CIB3. It placed a bug in the offices of Southern Investigations that yielded evidence that convicted Rees for a serious and unrelated crime. Police surveillance shows frequent contact between Rees and Marunchak. I understand that the tapes made by the recording by the bug have not all been transcribed; if they were, they would yield more collusion, perhaps criminal in nature, between News International and Jonathan Rees. I hope the Minister will ask the police if that process is under way.

When Rees came out of jail, he was re-hired by the *News of the World*, then edited by Andy Coulson. Rees also founded a company called Pure Energy, in which Marunchak was involved. The police hold evidence to suggest that Rees discussed the use of Trojan devices with his associate, Sid Fillery. He was an associate of Philip Campbell Smith, who received a custodial sentence on Monday for a crime related to blagging. Campbell Smith is a former Army intelligence officer. I will say no more on Campbell Smith, because I do not want to prejudice the Operation Tuleta inquiry. However, I hope that I have demonstrated to the Minister a close association between Rees and Marunchak.

This is why I think that the Metropolitan police cannot be used in any further investigations: yesterday, the Leveson inquiry heard a startling revelation that Alex Marunchak—a close business associate of Jonathan Rees, then the prime suspect in a murder case—chose to put DCI David Cook and his family under close covert surveillance. The person who was investigating a murder was put under close surveillance by a close business associate of the man he was investigating. That was raised with Rebekah Brooks in 2002, the then editor of the *News of the World*. I would like the Minister to imagine what his response would have been to that information. A journalist employee tried to undermine the murder investigation of his close associate. Rupert Murdoch claims that News International takes a zero-tolerance approach to wrongdoing. However, far from launching a wide-scale inquiry to investigate wrongdoing, Rebekah Brooks promoted Alex Marunchak to the editor's job at the *News of the World* in Ireland.

It gets worse. Last year, Mr Cook's then wife, Jacqui Hames, discovered that her records appeared in the evidence file of Glenn Mulcaire. The records show information that she believes could only have been obtained from her private police records. While DCI Cook was investigating a murder, his colleagues in another part of the Met were in receipt of evidence that a close associate of his suspect was illegally targeting him. Did Andy Hayman, the then head of the hacking inquiry, who also happened to be in charge of the fourth investigation into Daniel's murder, ensure that his colleague was informed about this? No. When Andy Hayman retired early from the Met, he became a paid contributor for News International—that is not right. For months, Scotland Yard took no action. Why not? Why was it not willing to pursue what appears to be a clear attempt to interfere with the murder inquiry of Daniel Morgan?

The Guardian has reported that the reason why no action was taken by Scotland Yard was not to embarrass the Met with newspapers.

It gets worse. I would like the Minster to request to see all the intelligence reports submitted about Alex Marunchak. I believe the Met is sitting on an intelligence report from late 2002 that claims a police contact overheard Marunchak claim he was paying the relatives of police officers in Cambridgeshire for information about the Soham murders. As far as we know, those allegations have not been investigated. I do not know whether the intelligence reports are accurate, but I do know that Alex Marunchak was involved in writing stories about how the Manchester United tops of those young girls were found. I also believe that at least one of the Soham parents appears in the evidence file of Glenn Mulcaire. The Met police failed to investigate both leads when reported in 2002 and 2006. I think that Rupert Murdoch owes the Morgan family an apology, and I do not think that he has made his last apology to the grieving parents of murdered children.

Daniel's family will never see his murderer brought to justice—corruption at the Metropolitan police has ensured that—but the Minister has it in his power to see that they get an explanation of the failure. He can only do that if the next investigation has their confidence. They seek a judge-led inquiry into the police's handling of the murder, because they have lost confidence in the police. In the circumstances, wouldn't anyone?

APPENDIX E

Review into Operation Abelard II by the Crown Prosecution Service and the Metropolitan Police Service
May 2012

1. Introduction

1.1 In March, 2011, three men were acquitted on a charge of murder, following a decision by the Crown to offer no evidence against them. This decision was reached following many months of pre trial hearings. In the year preceding the final acquittals, the Crown had already offered no evidence in respect of 2 other defendants, one of whom had been charged with murder and the second with perverting the course of justice.

1.2 The murder trial related to that of Daniel Morgan, a man who had been killed twenty-four years earlier, in March, 1987. The factors and circumstances which gave rise to the decision to withdraw the prosecution have their origins in a multiplicity and complexity of criminal investigations which have spanned over two decades.

1.3 Six criminal investigations have focused on Daniel Morgan's murder. Operation Abelard II was the name given to the most recent investigation into the murder of Daniel Morgan, and which led to the charges in this case being brought. Additionally a number of separate police enquiries developed which were linked to his death. These lengthy police enquiries involved Hampshire Constabulary, the Police Complaints Authority and the MPS Directorate of Professional Standards (DPS).

1.4 In the last twenty years over sixty people have been arrested, (some individuals more than once), twelve were for murder. Three of these people were charged in 1989 before their case was also withdrawn. A chronology of the relevant investigations, reviews and arrests are shown at Appendix A.

1.5 It is against this background and following the unsuccessful prosecution that this Review was commissioned in order to allow police and prosecutors to identify the precise reasons which culminated in the prosecution offering no evidence in this case. The Terms of Reference apply only in relation to Operation Abelard II and are set out in paragraph 1.11 below.

1.6 Having identified the issues that led to the Crown offering no evidence in this case, the additional purpose of this Review was to identify any good practice and learning points that police officers and prosecutors could benefit from in the future. The process of a post case evaluation is recognised as good practice, particularly in complex prosecutions.

1.7 As will be clear from the Terms of Reference below, the purpose of commissioning this Review was not to investigate allegations of corruption, nor was it intended to serve the purpose of an investigation for police disciplinary purposes.

1.8 The joint Review was commissioned by the Crown Prosecution Service (CPS) and Metropolitan Police Service (MPS). Two factors directly contributed to the Crown's difficulties in prosecuting the case. These related to the unreliability of critical witnesses, (particularly non-adherence to the handling protocols of one of those witnesses), together with difficulties in meeting the demands of disclosure. Whilst both these factors were recognised by police and prosecutors as the pre-trial hearings progressed, there are, nevertheless, important lessons to be drawn from the proceedings and which are considered pertinent for any future investigations and prosecutions.

1.9 This Review has thus examined the two central matters, namely; the management and use of witnesses under the Serious Organised Crime and Police Act, 2005 (SOCPA) and the Disclosure of Unused Material. During the review two further areas for improvement were identified; namely the archiving of police material and the control and direction of the investigation and prosecution.
1.10 Terms of Reference were established by Chief Crown Prosecutor, CPS London, Alison Saunders and Assistant Commissioner Cressida Dick, MPS.
1.11 Terms of Reference:

(i) Examine the methodology, decisions and tactics used by the prosecution team (police and prosecutors) to deal with the witnesses who were given agreements pursuant to the SOCPA legislation.

(ii) Examine the methodology, decisions and tactics adopted by the prosecution team (police and prosecutors) in order to discharge their disclosure obligations, (to include any omissions).

(iii) Consider any other significant key areas which may emerge during the course of the review

(iv) To make recommendations in relation to any lessons learnt or good practice which emerge from the review.

2. Methodology

2.1 A range of opinions and concerns were expressed during the Review and those matters, together with the significant number of decisions and Judge's Rulings made during the course of the prosecution have been noted.

2.2 Commander Simon Foy (MPS) and Deputy Chief Crown Prosecutor Jenny Hopkins (CPS) interviewed the following key members of the Abelard II prosecution team:

2.3 Lawyers	Interview date
Stuart Sampson - Reviewing Lawyer – CPS	14.06.2011
Nicholas Hilliard QC - Lead Counsel	22.06.2011
Jonathan Rees QC - Junior Counsel	12.10.2011
Heather Stangoe - Disclosure Counsel	26.07.2011

2.4 MPS /SOCA	
David Cook - Senior Investigating Officer (SIO)	11.07.2011
DCI Noel Beswick - Deputy SIO	07.07.2011

DI Doug Clark - SOCPA liaison officer for investigation team   10.10.2011
DS Gary Dalby - Case Officer   05.07.2011
DI Tony Moore - De-brief Manager   14.07.2011
DI Bernard Greaney – Directorate of Professional Standards   03.08.2011
Former Assistant Commissioner John Yates   .   22.12.2011

3. Background

3.1 Daniel Morgan, a private investigator, was murdered on the 10th March 1987. He had been struck several times with an axe whilst in the car park of the Golden Lion public house, Sydenham Road, Lewisham. The motivation for the murder was never sufficiently established, thus theory and speculation developed. Nevertheless, what is clear is that Daniel Morgan was a business partner with William Jonathan Rees and both worked within their company named Southern Investigations.

3.2 Operation Abelard II commenced in March 2006. It brought together all the material from the previous investigations and sought to secure evidence which could identify and successfully prosecute any person. The volume of material that had already been gathered was extensive and the following years would create even more. All of the material was subsequently required to be considered for disclosure.

3.3 By 2008 a sufficiency of evidence existed to charge five men, namely; William Jonathan Rees, James 'Jimmy' Cook, and brothers Garry and Glenn Vian with the murder of Daniel Morgan. The fifth, Sidney Fillery, (a serving police officer in 1987 and an associate of William Jonathan Rees) was charged with perverting the course of justice, viz interfering with the investigation into the murder of Daniel Morgan.

3.4 The CPS decision to charge followed careful consideration of all the evidence. It is pertinent to note the observation of the Judge, Mr Justice Maddison, in March 2011 when he stated:-
"...there is no doubt, it seems to me, that given the evidence available to the police before these proceedings were instituted the police did have ample grounds to justify the arrest and the prosecution of the defendants..."

3.5 The prosecution relied on many witnesses but a number were crucial to the prosecution. The Crown's case was clear with regard to the alleged individual culpability of the five defendants, and whilst the names cannot be fairly ascribed here, in light of the subsequent acquittals, evidence was to be produced which the Crown considered demonstrated;

(i) who actually killed Daniel Morgan,

(ii) who drove the get-away car,

(iii) who provided assistance on the night of and subsequently after the murder,

(iv) who paid and arranged for the murder

3.6 Among the witnesses, the Abelard II investigation team secured three who were debriefed under the provisions of SOCPA. It is a fundamental requirement when using assisting offenders that the prosecuting authorities are satisfied with the integrity of those witnesses.

3.7 It was within this domain, together with that of disclosure issues, that the Crown's case became undermined.

3.8 The main reason for the withdrawal of the prosecution was the Crown's inability to fully satisfy their disclosure obligations. However at this time there were also issues with the reliability of key prosecution witnesses. The disclosure difficulties were the dominant factor and were the more impactive. These two issues are reported on in more detail below.

4. Disclosure

4.1 The Criminal Procedure and Investigations Act 1996 (CPIA), as amended by the Criminal Justice Act 2003, requires the prosecution to disclose all material that might reasonably be considered capable of undermining the prosecution case against the accused or of assisting the case for the accused.

4.2 Under the Code of Practice, that accompanies the CPIA, material is defined as 'relevant' if it appears to the investigator, officer in charge of an investigation or the disclosure officer to have '…some bearing on any offence under investigation, or any person being investigated, or on the surrounding circumstances unless it is incapable of having any impact on the case'

4.3 The CPIA imposes statutory duties on the police and prosecutors in relation to the handling of unused material and in particular the obtaining and retaining of material, its inspection and disclosure. Although this case pre-dated the implementation of the CPIA, the view was taken that the common law rules (which preceded the CPIA) were, for all practical purposes, in line with the CPIA. This view was endorsed by Mr. Justice Maddison at a hearing on 17th July 2009. It should be noted that under the common law there was no requirement for the defendants to provide the Prosecution with Defence Case Statements.

4.4 A pertinent paragraph within the Code for Crown Prosecutors states:

"Prosecutors must make sure that they do not allow a prosecution to start or continue where to do so would be seen by the court as oppressive or unfair so as to amount to an abuse of the process of the court." (Paragraph 3.5)

4.5 A trial will only be a fair one if the prosecution are able to discharge their disclosure obligations in relation to the retention, recording and revelation of material. It is within this legal framework that the police team faced a considerable challenge.

4.6 From the outset it was recognised that not only had a vast amount of material accumulated over 23 years, (estimated at 750,000 pages) but it was material that had been gathered by different investigation teams within the Metropolitan Police, other agencies such as the Forensic Laboratories, Crown Prosecution

Service and Police Complaints Commission and police forces, national enforcement and intelligence agencies (Hampshire Constabulary, Regional Crime Squad, National Criminal Intelligence Service). Some of the material was only available in physical documents - having been collated before the capability to store such material electronically and was retained at a variety of locations.

4.7 An appreciation of the scale and complexity of the disclosure issues in this case is essential to understanding why the prosecution offered no evidence. At Appendices C, D and E are three key rulings of Mr Justice Maddison, in which the issues of disclosure are addressed in considerable detail. The dates of the rulings are; December 2009, March 2010 and March 2011. The first two rulings (Appendices C and D) relate to applications to extend the custody time limits (CTLs) of the defendants. The first ruling (C) being made during the course of an extensive voire dire. It was alleged by the defence that the prosecution had failed in their disclosure obligations, and therefore they had not acted with due diligence and expedition and thus the defendants should be released on bail. The nature of this case, and in particular the involvement of SOCPA witnesses, led to a requirement for specific and detailed disclosure relating to those witnesses. In seeking to meet those obligations further and more detailed material was necessary to be discovered and disclosed.

4.8 It should be noted that Appendix C is an edited extract of Mr Justice Maddison's ruling of 18th December, 2009. In addition to explaining the background and complexity of the case the ruling sets out fifteen separate matters in which the Crown had, so claimed the Defence, failed in their disclosure obligations. The ruling articulates the Judge's findings in respect of each of those matters.

4.9 Whilst the reader is directed to Appendix C to fully appreciate the extent and scale of the disclosure arguments, the summary below sets out the fifteen disclosure issues as raised by the defence and the Judge's decision in respect of each of them.

4.10 The referencing relates, firstly, to the page & initial line number of each disclosure argument, followed by the page and initial line reference for the Judges' decision. The reader can go directly to that passage in Appendix C to see fuller detail.

4.11 Summary of alleged disclosure failings. Ruling of 18th December, 2009.

1. Failure to fully disclose a 2006 Metropolitan Police Authority report relating to the Morgan murder.

1a. *Upheld. Document should have been disclosed. There was no answer for the failure.*

2. Inappropriate redactions to some transcripts of debriefed SOCPA witnesses.

2a. *Upheld. The documents were inappropriately redacted. However by date of this ruling the defence did have the unredacted versions.*

170

3. Complaint relating to Dr Chesterman's psychiatric report relating to Witness B. Insufficient attention given to contents of the Witness Protection Unit comments.

3a. *Complaint has little merit, if any at all. Not a complaint about lack of disclosure.*

4. Complaint relating to the late disclosure of variety of police documents – e.g. reports, notebooks, messages, etc. p82, line 22.

4a. *Full significance of these documents would not have been apparent, until detailed written defence submissions received. Not regarded as a failure to disclose.*

5. Late disclosure relating to Witness L, specifically that regarding the witnesses' integrity and credibility.

5a. *Upheld. The defence had a perfectly legitimate point - the material should and could have been disclosed before 5.10.2009.*

6. Prosecution disclosure counsel informed defence that police were unaware of any psychiatric issues relating to Witness B, between 26th July and 6th September 2006.

6a. *Upheld. There is no answer to the Defence point made.*

7. Late and unduly late disclosure of general practitioner records relating to Witness B.

7a. *Upheld. Judge considered they could and should have been disclosed.*

8. Failure to provide information of medical records of Witness B, in relation of stroke he had suffered.

8a. *The point viewed as having no real merit. The request came "late in the day" and was responded to relatively quickly.*

9. Late discovery and disclosure by police of papers relating to the prosecution of Witness W.

9a. *Judge concluded that 'first appearances' were deceptive in this matter. Whilst there seemed to have been a clear breakdown in disclosure process, that was not the position. Despite initial extensive searches failing to retrieve the documents they were discovered and disclosed.*

10. Witnesses present at the Golden Lion public house on night of murder. Defence claim that prosecution failed to supply the relevant details and defence had to instruct private investigators to ascertain details.

10a. *Judge did not detect any lack of due diligence or expedition. The police made enquiries, traced witnesses and disclosed details to the defence. Not a case where disclosure was held back.*

171

11. Non-disclosure of a statement relating to Mr Haslam.

11a. *Upheld. The circumstances in which the document was discovered indicated a failure in the disclosure process.*

12. A failure to provide prison records, record of visits and phone call of the defendant Mr Rees.

12a. *Judge's view that there were no material documents of the kind sought, that should be disclosed.*

13. Defence requests made in October 2009 regarding matters within the statement of Mr Haslam.

13a. *Whilst acknowledging there was confusion over reference numbers, the Judge upheld the view that there was some failure in the disclosure process.*

14. Defence complaint concerning method of disclosure of telephone records, between defendant Mr Rees, the deceased and a Paul Goodridge, in which the subscriber details were obscured.

14a. *The Judge considered that there had been no lack of due diligence of expedition. The defence had detected the problem, informed the prosecution and the remedy was immediately provided to ensure the details were revealed.*

15. Defence complaint that following service of all graphics on 25th February 2009, they were served with other graphics in December 2009, relating to photographs taken in 2007.

15a. *These photographs were taken twenty years after the murder. Could neither assist the defence or undermine the prosecution. Considered need not have been disclosed at all.*

4.12 The above matters illustrate the immense detail that was continually being undertaken during the pre-trial process to address the disclosure issues. It should be noted that the December 2009 ruling followed from an earlier one, heard in April 2009, in which the Common Serjeant of London had concluded that;

"....the prosecution had in fact conducted themselves with due diligence and expedition despite certain failings on their part in relation to disclosure, having regard to the size and complexity of the case".

4.13 Mr Justice Maddison equally concluded that the Crown had acted with due diligence and expedition and ruled that the custody time limits would be extended. The Judge's comments on this matter are shown in full at pages 99 - 107 of Appendix C. In his view the "scale and the complexity" of the case were critical factors in reaching his decision. It is pertinent to set out one part of his observations;

"on any fair view it seems to me that disclosure has been and continues to be a formidable, daunting exercise. ... ... The extraordinary nature of the case has required the prosecution to undertake an exercise in disclosure of exceptional if

not unprecedented proportions. They have had to consider what documents to disclose relating not only to the most recent investigation, itself of great length and complexity, but relating to all four earlier investigations. They have had to examine documents covering a period of more than 20 years. I am told that more than 500,000 pages of material have been examined in this connection".

4.14 Thus, by December 2009, the Crown had twice demonstrated that they were acting with due diligence and expedition and were meeting their disclosure obligations correctly, albeit with some individual failings, but none so great as to affect the case.

4.15 However, at the time of the December 2009 ruling, a further disclosure issue had already arisen but which had not formed part of the submissions relied upon by the Defence in their attempt to secure their clients' release from custody. This was because they had not been informed of the development.

4.16 This new issue related to additional crates of material being discovered which subsequently proved to have a bearing and relevancy to the defendants' case. As will be noted above, Points 5, 6, 7 and 9 also related to the 'late discovery' of material and thus this new matter greatly concerned Mr Justice Maddison.

4.17 In a further ruling by Mr. Justice Maddison, on 3rd March 2010, the Judge sets out what he described as "a highly complex sequence of events in a case in which frankly nothing seems to be straightforward". Whilst the Judge's succinctness and summation of the issues cannot be bettered here and only a reading of his ruling will inform the reader of the full facts, it is necessary to explain some of the detail below. (Appendix D shows the full ruling.)

4.18 In 2007, during the earliest stage of Abelard II, the investigation team learned of possibly relevant material that was located in crates at the offices of the Directorate of Professional Standards (DPS), in Putney. Operation Abelard II officers examined the boxes (believed some 15 or 17 crates) and established that the papers related to a money laundering investigation undertaken by DPS, from 1999, in which two of the current defendants, one of the SOCPA witnesses and three other people were investigated. However, since the 1999 investigation had not proved the money to be illicit proceeds under the Drug Trafficking Act no prosecution was possible.

4.19 The money laundering investigation was already known to the Abelard II investigation team and a full CPS advice file was in their possession. It is clear that at this stage the investigation team had not fully appreciated the significance of this material and a decision was made by the SIO that the material was not relevant. Thus the crates, which in fact never came to the enquiry team's office, were returned by the DPS for storage. With hindsight, this decision has been recognised as incorrect, since the crates contained some material which failed to be disclosed. Following their return to storage, the crates were not seen again until November 2009.

4.20 By early 2009 it became necessary for further enquiry to be made of Witness W, who had become a significant witness in the case. His evidence was regarded as critical but was strongly disputed by the defence, who claimed

Witness W was wholly unreliable. Hence the need to locate any case papers which related to Witness W became pressing.

4.21 In addition to seeking material in respect of Witness W, the investigation team also sought further material relating to Witness A. In an attempt to discover such material a further visit by Abelard II officers was planned of the DPS offices. As a result of this proposed visit the DPS identified eighteen crates which they believed might contain relevant material. This late discovery was on 16th November, 2009, a month prior to the custody time limit argument of 18th December, 2009.

4.22 These newly discovered crates were in fact the very same crates that had been placed in storage in 2007, having been regarded as irrelevant at that time. However, this fact was not immediately appreciated by the investigating officers. Only upon detailed examination of the crates' contents was it appreciated that there was material pertinent to both Witness A and W.

4.23 The significance of this new material was not lost upon the Deputy Senior Investigating officer. He immediately reported the discovery to prosecution disclosure counsel and informed prosecution counsel by email. He wrote a further email to the DPS, seeking an explanation for the late discovery - still unaware that the crates were the ones already 'viewed' some two years earlier.

4.24 Neither the Judge nor defence counsel were made aware of the finding of the 18 crates prior to the custody time limit argument of 18th December, 2009. Whilst the content of the crates had been initially assessed, the significance of the material (namely that some of it met the disclosure test) was not appreciated until March 2010.

4.25 Mr Justice Maddison ruled in March 2010 that these latest revelations were, in his view, "a sorry tale". He commented that "...in essence, and this is the heart of the matter,... the prosecution are only now in the process of disclosing material which is properly disclosable which has been discovered in crates of which they were aware but which they decided not to inspect in the middle of 2007".

4.26 Aligned to the above discovery was the fact that, coincidentally, additional and relevant disclosable material, relating to Witness W was also recovered from another DPS premises in Ilford. The defence were informed of the fact of the Ilford discovery and appropriate disclosure was made to them prior to the 18th December 2009 CTL hearing.

4.27 Mr Justice Maddison ruled that the prosecution had demonstrated a lack of due diligence and expedition and accordingly he declined to extend the custody time limits. All the defendants were released on bail. He did however state *"I should like to make it clear that I have no reason to believe that I or the defence counsel were deliberately misled".*

4.28 Two further matters then arose. During January 2011, upon clearing office premises that previously belonged to the DPS in Penrhyn Road, Kingston, papers were recovered that related to Witness A. These papers dealt with Witness A's role as an informant but in another pseudonym. Not only did they show that

174

Witness A had been providing contradictory evidence to that contained within his formal SOCPA debriefing (and thus his credibility was damaged) but until the discovery the investigation team knew nothing of the matter.

4.29 The second matter arose during a voire dire in February 2011. The defence had been provided with copies of relevant emails of the then Assistant Commissioner John Yates. Additionally they had been provided with a copy of the internal DPS report which explained the movement of the eighteen crates. As part of their continuing request for material, the defence sought access to particular documents stored within the eighteen crates and made specific reference to Box numbers. The police team were unable, in respect of four of the boxes, to locate them.

4.30 Whilst one of the four crates contained material which bore no relevance to the trial proceedings, the other three did. They related to the money laundering case previously referred to. It became apparent that there had been a clear oversight in respect of these three crates. Whilst they were already within the police Exhibit's room, they had not been entered in to the police records, nor ever assessed. This was clearly an error. These three crates had gone unnoticed and were overlooked, whilst stored amongst many other crates.

4.31 The third court transcript, that of 11th March, 2011, (see Appendix E) sets out the Crown's final position and explains briefly the 'four crate issue' and the discovery of material at Penrhyn Road.

4.32 These latest developments proved to be the final undoing and the cumulative weight against the Crown's position became untenable. The police determined that it was no longer possible to be sure that they were able to account for all the relevant unused material that had been generated both in the course of Operation Abelard II and the preceding operations. The effect of this conclusion was that the Crown were no longer able to be confident they could discharge their disclosure obligations and they would have to offer no evidence against the defendants.

4.33 Leading counsel for the Crown, Mr Hilliard QC, explained to the Court, that;

"the task of investigating and preparing this case has been immense and unrelenting". Further, he acknowledged, "..the prosecution accept that we cannot be confident that the defence in this particular case necessarily have all the material to which they are entitled".

4.34 Mr. Justice Maddison, in recognising the position, made the following observations:

"I endorse the view that you have expressed, that the recent enquiry in relation to the 18 crates and the recent discovery of the four further crates do give rise to a general sense of uncertainty as to whether the disclosure process in this highly unusual case can in truth ever properly be carried out".

4.35 He went on to say; *"I think it correct to add that in my view the decision that you have taken is not only principled but it is right". He said "In all the*

175

years that I have been a judge, and there are many, many of them, I have never come across a case in which there have been so many issues or such complex issues to be resolved before a trial could even get underway".

4.36 By the time the final disclosure difficulties were revealed, the case had already been significantly weakened by the fact that the three SOCPA prosecution witnesses had been withdrawn from the prosecution case. Those issues are now explained.

5. Management and use of SOCPA witnesses

5.1 There were three witnesses who were the subject of the SOCPA regime, in this case, who were regarded as significant to a successful prosecution. Each had a considerable bearing on the investigation and prosecution. These three witnesses are referred to here by their pseudonyms and are dealt with in the order with which they entered the investigation:

Witness A

Witness B

Witness C

5.2 Each witness raised different issues but for different reasons, all came to be regarded as unreliable witnesses and for whom the prosecution could no longer depend for their veracity in this prosecution. With regard to Witness A their unreliability emerged through the late discovery of material as described at paragraphs 4.21 - 4.35. Further, with Witness B, there were handling irregularities and issues which affected his credibility. Witness C was not subject to any late disclosure issues and in fact Witness C's unreliability arose solely because of the correct approach and detailed enquiry made by Abelard II officers during the pre-trial period. It should be noted two of the SOCPA witnesses were not in custody for the duration of the de-brief process. (Witnesses B and C). The Court transcripts (Appendices C,D,E) provide further detail as to the role and importance of these witnesses.

5.3 Witness A

5.4 Witness A entered the SOCPA de-brief process in May 2006. He had known one of the defendants for many years and both had dealt in drugs together since 1989. Witness A was subsequently introduced to two of the other defendants.

5.5 Witness A was told that one of the defendants would do favours, such as gaining information from the police. Witness A learned through his conversations who, allegedly, had committed the murder and who drove the car away. He also learned, allegedly, who had been participatory to the crime and who had, allegedly, 'ordered' the murder.

5.6 Witness A was in prison at the time he volunteered his evidence. He was given an agreement pursuant to s.73 SOCPA and de-briefed between May and December 2006. His criminal background was checked, including his status as an informant.

176

5.7 However not all of the informant files relating to this witness had been correctly archived. He had been registered with different law enforcement agencies, on several different occasions and in different names. Whilst all possible checks were completed by the investigation team there was no way of them knowing about an un-archived extract from an informant file which was subsequently found under a different pseudonym. (see paragraph 4.29).

5.8 Witness B

5.9 Witness B entered the enquiry in July 2006, following a newspaper appeal about the murder. Witness B was an associate of those who worked at Southern Investigations. Witness B and allegedly one of the defendants were involved in various criminal enterprises including drug trafficking. Witness B reported that in 1987 he had been asked to kill Daniel Morgan but he had refused.

5.10 Witness B claimed that he was a witness to the crime and had been invited to the Golden Lion public house on the evening of the murder. Witness B identified two of the defendants at the pubic house and he said that he saw Daniel Morgan. Witness B states he spoke to a number of the defendants at the public house on the night of the murder.

5.11 Witness B stated he saw two of the defendants in a car in the car park of the pub. He claims he saw Daniel Morgan's body lying in the car park. He was the prosecution's only eye witness to the murder.

5.12 Witness B claimed that his motive in coming forward was not financial but because he was worried about the safety of his family and he wanted to clear his conscience. He was de-briefed over many months between August 2006 and December 2007, during which time he admitted to many very serious crimes. These offences were dealt with separately and he pleaded guilty to twenty serious offences and asked for a further thirty one other offences to be taken into consideration for the purposes of sentence. He received an initial custodial sentence of twenty eight years imprisonment but this was reduced to three and a half years imprisonment.

5.13 During the de-brief Witness B was not in custody and this factor made it extremely difficult for the Witness Protection Unit (WPU), the de-briefers and the investigation team to manage him. He frequently disregarded the rules of the de-brief process and breached the requirement that the witness only deal with the debriefing team. He regularly contacted the Senior Investigating Officer directly.

5.14 Witness B was a difficult individual who had previous mental health issues. During the de-briefing process he was offered an appropriate adult but was adamant he did not want anyone else knowing about this process and refused their assistance.

5.15 Following the decision of the prosecution to offer no evidence in this case Mr Justice Maddison provided a careful and detailed ruling as to why Witness B's evidence would have been excluded. He provided this ruling due to a forthcoming trial where Witness B was a witness. There are a number of reasons given in the ruling but in summary they are:

(i) Breaches of the sterile corridor, i.e. the requirement for the witness to only have contact with the de-briefing team and not the investigative team;

(ii) The witness's mental health and the absence of an appropriate adult;

(iii) Witness B was (Mr Justice Maddison found) probably prompted by a senior police officer to implicate Glenn and Gary Vian;

(iv) Witness B had been tipped off that he had been caught lying about his father's death and given the chance to think of an explanation;

(v) The unreliability of Witness B as a witness including his significant criminal record;

(vi) His personality disorder which renders him prone to tell lies;

(vii) His differing and various accounts;

(viii) His demonstrative lies and his behaviour during the de-brief process.

5.16 Witness C

5.17 Witness C entered the enquiry as a witness at a much later stage and after the defendants had been charged. The witness was a close associate of one of the defendants and claimed to have been instructed not to speak to police.

5.18 In July 2009 Witness C made a statement detailing knowledge of the murder. The witness provided evidence about one of the defendant's alleged admissions regarding detail of the murder and other serious crimes. During Witness C's account there was further disclosure of being involved in serious criminality with the same defendant. The witness received a restricted use undertaking in October 2009 and was subsequently de-briefed.

5.19 Witness C had previously reported an assault case, whereby they were themselves the victim. The case against the attackers was subsequently dropped due to concerns about Witness C's evidence in relation to identification, location and timing. These concerns were confirmed by examination of mobile phone data which revealed an unsent draft of a text message, intended for the Witness Protection officer, relating to the assault, but timed some 8-10 hours before the alleged assault occurred.

5.20 It also transpired that Witness C was vulnerable and suffering from a post traumatic stress disorder due to issues from childhood. Although initially Witness C provided extremely credible evidence, as the de-brief continued evidence began to be exaggerated and the account kept changing. Extensive enquiries into the account provided gave considerable cause for concern.

5.21 Witness C went on to provide details in the de-brief regarding some thirty other murders. It was alleged these had been carried out by one of the defendants and his associates. Witness C gave an indication of burial sites in Epping Forest. Following detailed and extensive police searches at some of the sites indicated the Abelard II team then discovered that some of the information had been obtained by Witness C from a web-site on missing persons.

5.22 Subsequently the prosecution decided that they could no longer rely upon the evidence of Witness C. This decision was taken following concerns about the veracity of this witness, which were highlighted when police investigated further unrelated allegations made by the witness and which were found not to be credible.

6. Conclusion

6.1 By March 2011 the Crown no longer had the use of three critical witnesses. It was apparent that the case was, as Counsel described, "very finely balanced". The additional factor, that of the continuing disclosure problems, relating as it did to past investigations and witnesses, contributed to undermining the prosecution ability to guarantee full disclosure and fairness to the defendants.

6.2 However it was as a result of the disclosure difficulties that led, on 11th March 2011, Mr Hilliard QC to explain to the court that;

"the time has come when the prosecution no longer feel that we are able to satisfy the terms of paragraph 3.5 of the Code for Crown Prosecutors....it seems to us that that is now the inevitable conclusion to be drawn from the combination of matters outlined."

6.3 Recognition of this position was summed up by Mr Justice Maddison as follows;

"But the prosecution's case that remained in due course, after witnesses had fallen away, was dependent substantially, although not entirely, on witnesses of bad character and I am aware of the fact that the prosecution will have had to keep under constant review the strength of its own case and the likelihood ultimately of convictions".

7. Good Practice

7.1 This was a truly exceptional case in terms of a combination of factors namely its age; the size and the number of linked operations; the enormous volume of material generated, particularly unused, and the fact that all three of the SOCPA witnesses were undermined, post charge, by factors that adversely affected their credibility. In addition there was a lack of scientific evidence.

7.2 Further, it is important to note that whilst the murder of Daniel Morgan took place in March 1987, the Abelard II investigation was a continually developing one, with a new SOCPA witness coming forward post charge and new material being generated. This case presented challenges because the evidence in the case changed even between the decision to charge and the decision to offer no evidence.

7.3 The combination of all of these factors in one prosecution is a combination rarely likely to be encountered in prosecutions in the future.

7.4 The Review recognises that the handling of the SOCPA witnesses in this case is, to a limited extent, historic. In the intervening years since these SOCPA agreements were established, procedures and guidelines have evolved and reflect some of the good practice points below.

7.5 It is against this background that the following good practice is identified. Police and prosecutors in the future may benefit from following the Good Practice points that have applicability to their case. This Review makes a single over arching recommendation:

Recommendation

That steps are taken to disseminate this Review within the Police and CPS, so that Police and CPS can consider the following Good Practice points in future cases:

SOCPA witness issues

There is now a detailed ACPO guidance on the handling of SOCPA witnesses. It is recognised that certain aspects addressed in that document are equally dealt with here.

Good Practice Point 1

As a necessary pre condition to any future SOCPA agreement, the requirement for a thorough investigation addressing the credibility of the witness is paramount.

The following considerations would assist the police and prosecutors in respect of any potential SOCPA witness:

(i) Obtain and review all medical records

(ii) Obtain and review, (if any) all psychiatric records

(iii) Obtain and review all case papers regarding any previous convictions

(iv) Obtain and review all case papers regarding any previous investigations which did not lead to conviction

(v) Obtain and review all intelligence held by various investigative agencies regarding past and present criminality

(vi) Obtain and review all material regarding any past history as a 'CHIS'.

The timing of the review of this material will need to be carefully considered in each case. However we would recommend that there is a presumption in favour of reviewing this material prior to the entering into of a SOCPA agreement.

Good Practice Point 2

To maintain a full and auditable record of all police contact regarding the

management of any SOCPA witness.

During any investigation it is important to maintain a full 'record of contact log'. This will detail each and every single contact with the assisting offender, who instigated the contact and the reason for it.

This is particularly important to rebut allegations of inducing or coaching a witness, which may be made in court some considerable time after the contact in question. This will facilitate documentary accountability and demonstrate what contact or conversations did or did not occur between the investigations team, de-brief team and the witnesses, thereby obviating the necessity for lengthy voire dires.

Good Practice Point 3

Adherence to the following factors should be considered as 'best practice' when dealing with SOCPA witnesses.

   (i) A process to ensure effective control and regulation of the witness in terms of contact, allowances, privileges.

   (ii) A system to control the extent and duration of the de-brief. The parameters should be clearly set by a Gold group in conjunction with the SIO. There should be clear objectives to the process.

   (iii) Any Investigation team should be provided, (where possible) with regular and immediate transcripts of the de-brief (redacted if necessary), so that the investigation team can effectively challenge and corroborate what is being said in the de-brief.

   (iv) De-brief material should be edited for disclosure purposes on a continual basis, rather than edited at the end of the process.

   (v) A process for the investigation team to be able to provide questions to the de-brief team without breaching the 'Sterile Corridor' should be developed.

   (vi) A dedicated and separate de-briefing manager should be appointed to manage and supervise de-briefers.

   (vii) The De-brief team should be represented at the Gold Group.

   (viii) There is a need for parity of rank between investigative team's SIO and the leader of the de-briefing team. This will aid effective communication. At the very least this should be a relationship that is clearly defined, recorded and subject to inclusion within the terms of reference of the Group.

   (ix) The whole prosecution team (police, CPS, Trial Counsel) should take a pro-active role in the development and function of such witnesses. As it is the CPS who enter into the SOCPA agreement with the Assisting Offender, it is essential that the CPS are kept informed of developments with that witness.

(x) Consideration should be given of the benefits of the CPS lawyer dealing directly with the solicitors for a SOCPA witness.

(xi) Consideration should be given to the use of an appropriate adult for a SOCPA witness who may be vulnerable due to mental health issues.

Management of Disclosure

As already described, the issues surrounding disclosure were ultimately responsible for the withdrawal of the prosecution of Operation Abelard II. The following good practice points are set against this background and with an overriding consideration that historic cases, such as these, do not progress to charge stage unless and until the police and prosecutors are content that all relevant unused material has been identified and located and the initial disclosure exercise is complete.

Good Practice Point 4

Consideration needs to be given at the outset to the types of unused material that could reasonably expected to be encountered in a particular prosecution, and its anticipated location.

The parameters of the search for potentially relevant material need to be clearly documented.

This will enable the disclosure officer, senior investigating officer and lawyers to critically assess the material in their possession and assist in identifying any categories of material that they would expect to be generated in a particular investigation and which they are not in possession of. For example, Medical records, Informant files, DPS material, Microfiche records, General Registry files. The need for corporate memory cannot be underestimated and consideration should be given to locations and buildings previously occupied by law enforcement.

Good Practice Point 5

There is a requirement for accurate record keeping of all material which has been reviewed by the investigation during the enquiry and evaluated as not relevant together with detailed reasoning.

This should not be a schedule comprising the level of detail required in an unused disclosure schedule, but instead should be a record of what material was looked at in the course of the investigation and the decisions made in relation to it. This will mean that there is a record of the fact that the material exists, has been reviewed, the outcome of the review and its current location. What is required is an audit trail of what and when the material has passed through the hands of the enquiry team as well as CPS and counsel.

Good Practice Point 6

Consideration must be given to the size and complexity of the disclosure task from the outset. Consideration should be given to the level of experience required when appointing a disclosure junior.

Mr Justice Maddison made reference to the fact that the disclosure aspect of this case was far more challenging for the prosecution team than the evidential aspects of the case. This was a view shared by the prosecution team (police and prosecutors).

Traditionally the role of disclosure counsel is allocated to the most junior member of the counsel team. In the vast majority of cases this decision is entirely appropriate. However in exceptional cases such as this one, consideration should be given to the experience which disclosure counsel will need to possess and whether exceptionally a more experienced counsel is required.

Good Practice Point 7

The prosecution team (police and prosecutors) should frequently review the position and progress of the disclosure strategy.

The allocation of distinct roles and responsibilities to the reviewing lawyer and counsel in the prosecution team are essential to the effective progression of a case of this nature. Individuals will be frequently be under time constraints to deliver on their allocated task. It is therefore essential that effective and regular communication takes place between the individuals performing distinct roles. Communication between disclosure counsel and the rest of the prosecution team is vital. This is particularly important in cases such as this where the voire dires raised difficult and complex disclosure issues requiring the direct involvement of leading and junior counsel.

We suggest that it is good practice to arrange regular meetings, when updates can be provided by disclosure counsel to the team and when disclosure counsel's queries can be addressed.

Good Practice Point 8

Use of a Disclosure Strategy Document and clarity as to which disclosure regime applies.

The prosecution team in this case drafted a document entitled "Prosecution note on Disclosure" dated 29 July 2009. This note highlighted the fact that this was a pre CPIA case and set out how the prosecution were approaching disclosure, particularly in relation to the management of a huge volume of material and the tests to be applied to that material. This is to be viewed as good practice.

Prosecutors should draft a Disclosure Strategy Document for service on the court and defence. This document will set out the prosecution's approach from an early stage in relation to a number of matters, e.g. the application of the relevance test, the disclosure regime which applies, any key word searches being applied to bulk material and the handling of bulk material or digital material.

This will encourage the court and defence to engage in the disclosure process and highlight at an early stage any areas of disagreement, so that they can be resolved at an early stage.

In pre CPIA cases, identification of which disclosure regime will be applied, must be resolved as a priority post charge. An agreement must be reached with the defence, failing which an early ruling must be sought from the court. However it is recognised that such cases are becoming increasingly fewer.

Good Practice Point 9

Use should be made of the Criminal Procedure Rules to identify the issues in the case.

The requirement for the defence to provide a Defence Case Statement (DCS) only applies to cases governed by the CPIA. As this was a pre CPIA case DCSs were not required. The lack of DCSs created difficulties for prosecutors and the police in identifying the issues at an early stage. In cases which pre date the CPIA, prosecutors should utilise the Criminal Procedure Rules as a mechanism to encourage the defence to highlight the issues in the case.

Good Practice Point 10

Disclosure schedules need to be available electronically at court.

To assist the court and the smooth running of the case we recommend that it is good practice to scan all the disclosure schedules onto a laptop computer for use at court. This enables them to be easily searchable at court as issues arise.

Archiving Police documents

Good Practice Point 11

Ensure systems are in place to permit the identification and retrieval of all relevant material from historical operations. (e.g. informant files, microfiche, GR, DPS files, CPS case files).

A significant challenge in such historical cases is in ensuring that all relevant material has been found and reviewed. This task is made more complex by the use of different operational names when archiving, particularly when there are inter-linked investigations.

Considerable progress has been made within MPS archiving procedures to ensure that case papers and materials are archived correctly and where possible secured and recorded digitally.

When faced with a case of this nature it is recommended that a careful and considered judgment about the viability of being able to retrieve all material is made before a decision to proceed to charge is taken. This decision must be scrutinised, documented and recorded.

Control and Direction of Investigation/Prosecution

Good Practice Point 12

Historical and complex cases such as these should be structured within the governance arrangements and systems already in place within the MPS – primarily within the MPS Homicide & Serious Crime command.

Circumstances and events resulted in this case being managed outside the 'mainstream' governance systems already in place for the investigation of murder within the MPS. Whilst that may have had some merit and maintained confidentiality (considering the background to the case) it resulted in a complex management arrangement.

It is recommended that the governance arrangements (the MPS Gold Group structure) could and should have been able to consider matters of detail as appropriate e.g. the resolution of issues occurring during the management of the SOCPA witnesses above.
It is recommended therefore that any future investigation of this type should pay particular and detailed attention to the direction of the strategy - utilising the mechanisms already in place and in use within the MPS and as guided by MIRSAP and the MPS Murder Manuals.

Good Practice Point 13

The SIO should be employed by the police force that holds primacy for the enquiry. They are then directly accountable to the GOLD group and associated governance arrangements.

The SIO of the case retired from the MPS during the course of the investigation and was immediately re-employed by SOCA. Whilst he was still within the law enforcement arena and had a detailed knowledge of the case a full handover to a SIO who remained at the MPS would have been more appropriate. However it is recognised that this decision was made for sound reasons, particularly the SIO's detailed knowledge of this case and the strong relationship of trust he had developed with the family of Daniel Morgan.

Good Practice Point 14

Cases of this significance and complexity should be the subject of a CPS Case Management Panel

Case Management Panels were held in this case. The use of Case Management Panels is essential in a case of this type and is now a very well established practice. The panel is chaired by a senior lawyer, including the Director of Public Prosecutions or Chief Crown Prosecutor and their function is to oversee the effective progression of the prosecution, ensuring sound decision making and offering advice and guidance.

185

Good Practice Point 15

In protracted cases prosecution team succession planning should be considered.

Further to Recommendation 13, we recommend that the police and CPS consider succession planning for all members of the prosecution team. Such cases can take several years to reach court. It may be appropriate to appoint deputies for key members of the prosecution team, who will be able to assist both in busy periods and take over in the event that the relevant police officer or lawyer is absent or leaves the team.

Good Practice Point 16

Ensure there is a strategy in place to assist effective judicial case management.

A strategy is required to assist effective judicial case management throughout the duration of the case and adherence to the Criminal Procedure Rules. Case management hearings should utilise clear agendas, as identified in this case, as good practice.

In multiple defendant prosecutions there are likely to be extensive and repetitive oral legal arguments as between defendants. We recommend that the trial Judge is encouraged to rely on written advocacy, supplemented only where necessary by oral submissions. This will ensure hearings are focussed and court time is used efficiently. The prosecution should also encourage the management of the case through adherence to the Criminal Procedure Rules.

Good Practice Point 17

Appointment of a trial Judge.

Due to the category of charge in this case, namely murder, under the case release provisions, consideration had to be given to the appropriateness of releasing the proceedings from a High Court Judge to an authorised Senior Circuit or Circuit Judge. Owing to the complexities in this case it was retained by a High Court Judge. It will be important for the CPS to inform the court of all the complexities in a case, in order to ensure a Judge with the necessary experience is appointed.

Appendix A

Operation Abelard II - Time Line of events and linked investigations

10 March 1987 - Murder of Daniel Morgan
Daniel Morgan murdered. Death caused from multiple head injuries following assault with an axe, in the car park of the Golden Lion public house, Sydenham.

10 March 1987 - Operation Morgan
Murder investigation commenced by the Metropolitan Police (MPS). Led by

Detective Superintendent Douglas Campbell.

3 April 1987 - First arrests
Six men arrested in connection with the murder. Insufficient evidence to charge any person.

11 April 1988 - 25 April 1988 – Inquest held
Inquest at Southwark Coroner's Court. Coroner Sir Montague Levine. Verdict of 'unlawful killing' delivered. Following the inquest papers were re-submitted to the CPS. No charges were brought.

24 June 1988 - Concerns received from Daniel Morgan's family
Following concerns expressed by the victim's family, the investigation was voluntarily referred by the MPS to the Police Complaints Authority (PCA). A review commenced by Hampshire Constabulary. Terms of reference were: To investigate allegations that police were involved in the murder of Daniel Morgan and any other matters arising.

25 July 1988 - Operation Drake
Hampshire Constabulary commence enquiry in to the murder of Daniel Morgan, led by Detective Chief Superintendent Wheeler.

July 1988 - Operation Chagford
Secondary investigation by Hampshire Constabulary concentrating on the alibis of Paul Goodridge, William Jonathan Rees and Jean Wisden.

31 January 1989 - Arrests
Three people were arrested and charged by Hampshire Constabulary; - two for murder and one for perverting the course of justice.

11 May 1989
The Director of Public Prosecution discontinued proceedings, due to lack of evidence.

June 1989 - Operation Plymouth
Hampshire Constabulary enquiry overseen by the PCA. To investigate the allegation that police were involved in the murder of Daniel Morgan and any matters arising. The inquiry concluded there was no evidence to support any allegation of criminal misconduct by officers from the MPS.

1997 – January 1999 - Operations Landmark, Hallmark & Nigeria
MPS assessment and commencement of covert police investigations.

January 1999 - Operation Two Bridges
Additional MPS covert investigation examining police corruption and the murder of Daniel Morgan. Enquiry revealed information pertinent to the murder investigation. Charges brought in connection with an unrelated matter.

October 2001 - Murder Review Group (MRG)
MPS Murder Review Group examine Daniel Moran murder papers. New investigative opportunities identified and recommendation made that the case be re-investigated.

May 2002 - Operation Abelard
The MPS launched a fresh covert investigation into the murder of Daniel Morgan. Led by the Directorate of Professional Standards.

June 2002 - Operation Morgan II
MPS commence overt investigation of Daniel Morgan murder, in conjunction with Op Abelard. Includes CrimeWatch appeal, seeking new witnesses. Led by Detective Chief Superintendent Cook.

October 2002 - Jan 2003 - Further arrests
Eight arrests made in connection with the investigation. All persons released on bail.

March 2003 - CPS Advice
File submitted to the CPS for consideration of prosecution.

2 September 2003 - CPS decision
CPS determine that insufficient evidence for a prosecution. All eight suspects released from bail obligations.

September 2003 - Murder Review Group (MRG)
The MRG assessment concluded that all avenues of inquiry had been exhausted.

March 2006 - Operation Abelard II
MPS commence further murder investigation of Daniel Morgan's murder.

August - September 2006 - Arrests
Three men were arrested in connection with the murder. All bailed.

April 2008 - Charges laid.
    (i) The three returned on bail and were charged with murder;
       James Cook, Glenn Vian, Garry Vian.
    (ii) Two further men arrested in connection with the investigation.
       William Jonathan Rees subsequently charged with murder. Sid Fillery
       charged with perverting the course of justice.
    (iii) A serving police constable arrested on suspicion of misconduct in a public
       office. Officer bailed pending inquiries.

July 2008 - Plea & Case Management Hearing
Trial date set for April 2009. This date subsequently vacated.

September 2008 – No Further Action to be taken re a Police Officer
Serving police officer's bail cancelled. Decision for 'no further action'.
Officer suspended and subsequently resigned from the MPS.

December 2008 – Further arrest
A seventh man arrested on suspicion of attempting to pervert the course of justice.

March 2009
New trial date set for October 2009.

June 2009 - Further arrest
A woman was arrested on suspicion of conspiracy to murder. Person bailed.

October - December 2009 - Court proceedings
Pre-trial hearings - 'Abuse of Process' argument. Trial date vacated and provisionally fixed for 24 January 2011.

November 2009 – No Further Action of woman
The woman was released no further action.

March 2010 - Defendants Bailed
The defendants; William John Rees, James Cook, Glenn and Garry Vian all granted conditional bail. New trial date listed for November 2010.

Reporting restrictions were invoked by the judge.

2010 - Defendant discharged from trial
Case against James Cook withdrawn. Formally acquitted as Not Guilty.

October 2010
November trial date vacated. New date of 24 January 2011.

January - February 2011
Further pre-trial hearing and legal argument. Disclosure issues addressed.

March 2011
Additional disclosable material recovered by the MPS.

11 March 2011 - Defendant's discharged
Crown offer of evidence. Remaining three defendants formally acquitted.
William Jonathan Rees, Glenn Vian, Garry Vian.

APPENDIX F

Jacqui Smith's Letter to Sir Ian Blair

Home Office

HOME SECRETARY
2 Marsham Street, London SW1P 4DF www.homeoffice.gov.uk

Sir Ian Blair QPM Commissioner
New Scotland Yard Broadway
London SW1H OBG

0 2 OCT 2008

Thank you for coming to see me this morning to notify me of your intention to resign as Commissioner in two months time. I accept your decision with great regret.

You have been Commissioner at a time of unprecedented terrorist threat and have led the force in disrupting a series of plots as well as helping to bring many terrorists to justice. You led the Met through the dreadful events of the London bombings on 7th July 2005 and dealt with these with decisiveness and courage to bring the city back to normality. Two years later, I saw your immense contribution vividly on my first day in office at the time of the Haymarket attempted bombing. As Commissioner you have played a major role in shaping our national counter terrorism capability.

At the same time, you have secured significant falls in crime in London and have been at the fore front of the introduction of Neighbourhood Policing across the capital. Your contribution and drive to see these projects through were instrumental to their success and this leaves a lasting legacy.

You have faced the complex challenges of your office with unwavering commitment. It is the job of responsible politicians to support those who have to carry heavy operational burdens. It has been my honour to do so.

I want to extend my sincere gratitude to you and to your family for the service you have given London and the nation as Commissioner.

APPENDIX G

Jacqui Smith's Letter to Boris Johnson, Mayor of London

Home Office

HOME SECRETARY
2 Marsham Street, London SW1P 4DF www.homeoffice.gov.uk

Boris Johnson Mayor of London
Greater London Authority City Hall
The Queen's Walk More London London SE1 2AA

02 OCT 2OO8

Appointment of the next Metropolitan Police Commissioner

As you know, I have today received with regret Sir Ian Blair's decision that he will resign as Metropolitan Police Commissioner.

I am now putting in motion the process through which, as required by the Police Act 1996, I will recommend a new permanent appointment to Her Majesty. The Act provides that before recommending to Her Majesty that She appoint a person as Commissioner, I shall have regard to any recommendations made to me by the Metropolitan Police Authority and to any representations made to me by you personally as Mayor.

The office of Commissioner is an indispensable part of the good policing of London and of maintaining the national security of the country as a whole. I am sure we both agree that we need a process which will enable me to recommend the best person on merit for the office, having had regard to your and the Authority's views.

Accordingly, we need to invite applications from suitably qualified candidates. I would like the MPA to join with the Home Office in issuing this invitation.
Once applications have been received, the Home Office Permanent Secretary will lead a panel containing, I suggest, two MPA members which would then sift the applications and interview a short list. I am sure you and MPA members will then want to meet qualified candidates in order to form MPA views, and to enable you to make your own personal representation to me.

I would then interview one or more of the candidates before making my recommendation to Her Majesty.

My officials will be in touch with yours to set the process in motion.

APPENDIX H

Report into the Murder of Daniel Morgan
Commissioned by the Metropolitan Police Authority
Dated 27th October 2005

The murder of Daniel Morgan

Report: 10
Date: 27 October 2005
By: Chief Executive and Clerk

Summary

This report invites the Authority to consider whether it wishes to take steps in support of the Morgan family to investigate further into the events surrounding and subsequent to the murder of Daniel Morgan in 1987.

A. Recommendation

That the Authority decides whether it agrees to the proposals set out in paragraph 16 of this report.

B. Supporting information

The murder of Daniel Morgan

1. The following is a brief summary of the murder of Daniel Morgan and subsequent events. It does not reflect the complexities of this case or a number of the personalities involved. Nor can it do justice to the deep concerns that his family have about flaws in the conduct of the investigations into the murder and allegations that they have made publicly that police officers were involved in the murder itself.

2. In 1987 private investigator Daniel Morgan was murdered with an axe in a pub car park in Sydenham, south east London. At the time he was the business partner of Jonathan Rees in a company of private investigators called Southern Investigations. Jonathan Rees was regarded as the principal suspect. The primary motive was considered to be the circumstances surrounding a robbery at a Car Auction premises a year earlier.

3. Jonathan Rees undertook to provide security for the auctions, employing his brothers-in-law and three serving police officers, one of whom was DS Sidney Fillery. On 18 March 1986 the auction's takings were stolen in circumstances that led Belmont Auctions to conclude that Mr Rees had engineered the theft. As a result they sued Mr Rees and Mr Morgan through the civil courts. This caused a major breakdown in the relationship between the two partners and the MPS investigation team believed that this led to the murder.

4. Detective Superintendent Douglas Campbell led the MPS investigation team. Because the murder had occurred in the Catford police areas where he worked, DS Fillery was seconded to the murder squad. He failed to inform Mr Campbell of his association with Mr Rees or of his involvement with the Belmont incident. In addition he undertook a search of the offices of Southern Investigations,

allegedly removing a file relating to the Belmont Auctions work that was never seen by the investigation team. As soon as his role in the incident was discovered he was removed from the squad but Mr Campbell's view was that he had already fundamentally undermined the investigation.

5. In April 1987 Mr Rees, DS Fillery and the other two officers were arrested upon suspicion of being involved in the murder. All were later released uncharged.

6. In the following months there were rumours and allegations of high level police corruption and Masonic links surrounding the investigation but no charges resulted.

7. In April 1988 an inquest jury returned a verdict of unlawful killing. Daniel Morgan's family complained to the Police Complaints Authority about the conduct of the investigation and in June 1988 the Head of Hampshire CID undertook a review of the MPS investigation. His conclusion was that there was no evidence to suggest that police had been involved and that in his opinion Mr Rees had arranged the murder. Mr Rees was charged with this offence but the Director of Public Prosecutions subsequently discontinued the prosecution for lack of evidence.

8. In March 1988 Mr Fillery was medically discharged from the MPS and took Daniel Morgan's place as Mr Rees' partner at Southern Investigations.

9. In 1999 the MPS Anti-Corruption Command carried out a further investigation of Mr Rees' and Mr Fillery's alleged corrupt activities, together with the murder of Daniel Morgan. This found little evidence in relation to the murder but evidence of significant corruption. In addition, evidence was found of a conspiracy to plant cocaine on a young mother on behalf of her husband in order to win a custody battle for their child. As a result, in December 2000 Rees and the husband were sentenced to six years imprisonment, later increased to seven years on appeal.

10. The MPS Murder Review Group conducted a review of all available evidence and intelligence in 2001, followed by a focused re-investigation of the murder. This resulted in a report to the Crown Prosecution Service recommending that charges should be laid against various people. However, counsel's advice recommended that no charges should be pursued.

11. The current situation is that the murder is not being actively investigated but the case has not been closed. There therefore remains the chance that evidence may be forthcoming in the future that could lead to a prosecution and care should be taken not to prejudice this.

12. From the outset, Daniel Morgan's brother Alastair and other members of the family have consistently raised concerns over the police handling of this case (including the way that Hampshire Constabulary reviewed the first investigation) as well as alleging police officer involvement in the murder itself and subsequent collusion and cover up to a high level within the MPS. This case has been the subject of a great deal of media coverage over the years. The family's views are also represented on the website www.justice4daniel.org [1].

13. The family have received support over the years from MPs – including 57 MPs signing an Early Day Motion calling for a public judicial inquiry - and have met with the then Home Secretary, Jack Straw and more recently Hazel Blears. They have not, however, been successful so far in their main aim of getting agreement to the holding of a public inquiry into all the events surrounding this case.

The family's approach to the MPA

14. The family sought a meeting with Jennette Arnold, as their local MPA representative, and a meeting was subsequently held on 19 May 2005 between Jennette and Len Duvall, the Chair of the Authority, on behalf of the MPA, Alastair Morgan and other members of the family and supporting MPS. At this meeting Alastair Morgan and other family members briefed Len Duvall and Jennette Arnold on the events surrounding the case and their detailed concerns and reasons why they see a public inquiry as essential to restore confidence in the police and the criminal justice system.

15. The Chair undertook to reflect on the issues raised by the family and in what way the MPA might be able or prepared to act in the case towards securing a comprehensive account of what happened in the various investigations and a critique of the investigations. This would also give them support in their campaign. A further meeting with the family was held on 27 June at which the Chair outlined ways in which the MPA might be able and prepared to take action. Correspondence followed between the Chair, Alastair Morgan and the family's solicitor. The Chair also discussed the position with the MPS at a senior level. The Deputy Chief Executive & Solicitor has also met with Alastair Morgan and the family's solicitor to explore the options in more detail.

Proposals

16. It is the Chair's view that although this murder took place some 18 years ago, there are a number of unanswered questions which must continue to cast doubt on the integrity of the police service. He considers that an independent review, with a focused brief, would be a constructive and necessary way forward. On the basis of the Chair's discussions with the family the following steps are therefore proposed:

    i.   Under Section 22 (3) of the Police Act 1996, for the MPA to require the Commissioner to submit a Report to the Authority on the murder of Daniel Morgan and the subsequent investigations of that crime. The proposed commissioning brief for this report is set out in the appendix to this report. The Commissioner would be asked to prepare the report to be considered at the January 2006 meeting of the Authority in public session. The Report would be shared with the Morgan family and their comments obtained so that the Authority could consider those as well.

    ii.   Following consideration of the Commissioner's report, and in the light of comments from the family, the MPA will engage a barrister to independently review all the case papers in relation to the murder and all subsequent investigations. The barrister would be asked to produce a comprehensive appraisal of the several investigations and the various decisions by police and prosecuting authorities and to comment generally on the conduct of the investigations, and in particular to advise whether the case papers

        a.   Point to conclusions other than those reached by the most recent MPS review of the investigation

        b.   Indicate police corruption/collusion or involvement in either the murder itself or the subsequent failure of investigations

c.   Provide sufficient grounds to justify any prosecution

d.   Raise issues that could best be pursued through a public inquiry (for instance because of the power to summon witnesses) and what risks might flow from such an inquiry in relation to prospective prosecutions

The terms of reference of this review may be refined in the light of the Report by the Commissioner, taking account of views of the family of the deceased and the MPA.

The family of the deceased and the MPS will have opportunity to make written and oral submissions to the QC, and the MPS will be expected to respond to requests from the QC for further information.

This review would be conducted wholly in private. The QC's report would be made available to the family of the deceased.

Comments of the Deputy Chief Executive and Solicitor to the Authority

17. The Authority has no functions in relation to the investigation of the crime as such, or in relation to decisions whether or not to prosecute. Those are matters for the Commissioner and the prosecuting authority respectively.

However, in pursuing its responsibilities to secure effective and efficient policing, and to hold the Commissioner to account for the performance of the MPS, the Authority has a legitimate interest in receiving an explanation from the Commissioner of MPS' actions in the case. The Authority has the power to require a report from the Commissioner about past matters as well as present ones, and the power to obtain independent legal advice to assist it to come to a view on the conduct of the investigations as a matter of performance and learning.

The Authority does not have control of any of the papers relating to the investigations. The independent review by a barrister, as envisaged here, can only take place effectively with the full co-operation of the MPS in making documentation and evidential material available to the barrister in confidence. From discussions with the Deputy Commissioner and other Senior Officers it is understood that the MPS will give its co-operation.

Decisions

18. The Authority is therefore asked to decide whether it wishes to proceed in the way set out in paragraph 16. If agreed, the Authority would expect to receive the Commissioner's report at its January 2006 meeting, unless there were compelling reasons why this would not be possible. At this stage the Authority is being asked for an in principle decision in relation to an independent case review, pending an assessment of its likely scale and scope which will be informed by the contents of the Commissioner's report. Every effort will be made to contain the costs of the review within reasonable limits by focusing on the key questions whilst ensuring that the thoroughness of the review is not prejudiced.

C. Race and equality impact

There are no implications at this stage.

D. Financial implications

There are no financial implications at this stage, in that the Authority is being asked to make an in principle decision on an independent review. However, there would be significant financial implications if such a review was agreed and these would be addressed in a subsequent report.

E. Background papers

- Letter from the Chair of the Authority to Alastair Morgan, July 2005

F. Contact details

Report author: Simon Vile
For more information contact:
MPA general: 020 7202 0202
Media enquiries: 020 7202 0217/18

Letter from MPA Chief Executive & Clerk to Commissioner of Police of the Metropolis regarding the murder of Daniel Morgan

(this letter was sent after the full Authority meeting held on 27 October 2005 at which this report was presented)

3 November 2005
Sir Ian Blair, QPM, MA
Commissioner of Police of the Metropolis
New Scotland Yard

Dear Ian,

The murder of Daniel Morgan

As you know, the full Authority meeting last week considered whether it wished to take steps in support of the Morgan family in relation to the events surrounding and subsequent to the murder of Daniel Morgan in 1987.

Members decided, under Section 22 (3) of the Police Act 1996, to ask you to submit a report to the Authority, the commissioning brief for which is attached. This commissioning brief attempts to capture the concerns expressed by the Morgan family and I need to make it clear, therefore, that its wording does not imply that the Authority has formed any views about the several investigations of this murder in advance of receiving your report.

The Authority agreed to receive your report at its meeting on 26 January 2006. The Chair has undertaken to give the Morgan family sight of the report in sufficient time to allow them to submit written comments to Authority members. This suggests, therefore that your report should be completed, or substantially completed, by the end of December. I would be grateful if you could alert me at the earliest opportunity if this is not going to be possible, with your estimate of the timescale required for completion of a suitably comprehensive report.

The Authority intends to take your report in open session. I am, however, concerned to ensure that we do not prejudice any possibility of securing future convictions for this murder. Therefore, I would similarly welcome an early discussion if there are specific aspects that may need to be treated as exempt information. I would, however, expect the whole report to be made available to the Morgan family.

Following consideration of your report, and in the light of comments from the family, the MPA will consider whether to engage a barrister to conduct a thorough but focussed review of case papers in relation to the murder and the subsequent investigations. In the meantime, David Riddle will consult with AC Brown and David Hamilton as part of the MPA's consideration of the practical, legal and cost implications, and of a shortlist of Counsel who might be approached.

Yours sincerely
Catherine Crawford
Chief Executive & Clerk to the Authority

Appendix 1

Commissioning brief for a report to the Authority - issued by MPA pursuant to Section 22(3) of the Police Act 1996

To report on the murder of Daniel Morgan and the subsequent investigations of that crime, and specifically on:

1. the murder and the circumstances surrounding the murder
2. the first investigation of the murder carried out by the MPS – giving a comprehensive account of the investigation and its weakness including the possibility of the investigation being compromised and specifically covering

    a. the role of ex PS Sidney Fillery in that investigation: and

    b. the extent to which other police officers were amongst those who sought to protect him

3. The Coroner's inquest and verdict, including in particular the extent to which the inquiry was necessarily reliant upon the products of the first MPS investigation and therefore crippled by any identified weaknesses in that investigation (not least in relation to forensic evidence relating to the murder weapon and the integrity of the crime scene)

4. The further investigation by Hampshire Police, addressing in particular

    a. The extent to which the terms of reference of the investigation were changed whereby its focus was shifted away from its original purpose of investigating police involvement in the deceased's murder; and

    b. The extent to which the report of the investigation to the PCA on the question of police involvement in the murder was misleading in its findings, not least in relation to forensic evidence relating to the murder weapon and the integrity of the crime scene.

5. Subsequent reviews and re-investigation by the MPS, addressing in particular the circumstances in which the third investigation (The Two Bridges Inquiry) was conducted almost entirely without the knowledge of the deceased's family until it came to be aborted.

6. The extent of police corruption as it related to the murder of Daniel Morgan and the subsequent investigation

7. The current status of the inquiry
8. The lessons learned by the MPS from this case

The Commissioner's report will be made available to the family of the deceased.

APPENDIX I

A Partial Transcript of (former head of Anti-Corruption Command) Deputy Assistant Commissioner Bob Quick's Statement to the Leveson Inquiry

Operation Nigeria

During 1999, Anti-Corruption Command was conducting an operation, code named Operation Nigeria, which was a covert infiltration of office premises operated by 'Southern Investigations' whose proprietors were two men, Jonathan Rees ("Rees") and Sidney Fillery. Both were suspected of involvement in the murder of a former partner in the company, Daniel Morgan, who was murdered with an axe in a pub car park in
Sydenham in 1987. Fillery had been a former police detective and had worked on the original murder investigation. The objective of this operation was to try to advance the investigation into the Morgan murder. During the course of Operation Nigeria, it became clear that, amongst other criminal activities, 'Southern Investigations' was acting as a 'clearing house' for certain newspapers. Many of these stories were being leaked by police officers who were already suspected of corruption or by unknown officers connected to officers suspected of corruption, who were found to have a relationship with 'Southern Investigations'. A number of journalists were identified as having direct relationships with 'Southern Investigations'. To the best of my recollection these included journalists from papers like 'The Sun' and 'News of the World' but may
have included other newspapers. My recollection is that one of the journalists suspected was [Alex Marunchak]an executive with the 'News of the World'. During the operation it became clear that officers were being paid sums of between £500 and £2000 for stories about celebrities, politicians, and the Royal Family, as well as police investigations.

I recall one instance where certain officers from the Royalty Protection Branch appeared to have leaked a story in relation to a member of the Royal Family and details of bank accounts. It was often difficult to take direct action against such officers without compromising the covert investigation techniques being used against those connected with 'Southern Investigations', but where possible, action (criminal or discipline) was taken.

Matters in Operation Nigeria were brought to a head when evidence emerged that Rees was conspiring with a known criminal to plant cocaine on the criminal's wife in order to have her arrested and prosecuted so as to enable the criminal to win a custody battle over their one year old child. The Operation Nigeria investigation revealed that this conspiracy involved at least two corrupt Metropolitan Police detectives who were actively involved in attempting to pervert the course of justice in order to ensure the conviction and imprisonment of an innocent woman. These events precipitated the end of Operation Nigeria as police were forced to intervene and arrest those involved, thereby revealing that 'Southern Investigations' had been infiltrated covertly by police. Rees, two known criminals and two detectives were arrested and subsequently convicted and imprisoned for these crimes.

Report Recommending Investigation of Newspapers in 2000

Following these events and as a result of intelligence from Operation Nigeria, in around 2000, I wrote a short report highlighting the role of journalists in promoting corrupt relationships with, and making corrupt payments to, officers for stories about famous people and high profile investigations in the MPS. Despite detailed archive searches, the MPS have been unable to provide me with a copy; ordinarily material of this nature would have been destroyed after six years. In my report I recommended the commencement of an investigation into such activities. I believe my report also names some newspapers but I cannot recall which ones. I proposed an investigation of these newspapers/officers on the basis that I believed that the journalists were not paying bribes out of their own pockets but were either falsely accounting for their expenses and therefore defrauding their employers or, that the newspaper organisations were aware of the reasons for the payments and were themselves complicit in making corrupt payments to police officers.

I submitted my report to Commander Hayman ("Hayman"), who was at the time the head of MPS Professional Standards Department and the person I reported to directly. I recall speaking to Hayman about these matters and that he had reservations based on potential evidential difficulties pertaining to privileged material (journalistic material). I did not believe that the circumstances in which these stories were being obtained offered the facility to hide behind the legal protections available to journalists and I recall debating this with him. I am unable to say whether Commander Hayman referred this matter further up the command chain although I was under the impression he had. I did not sense much appetite to launch such an investigation although I felt Hayman was sincere in his reservations at the time. I do recall Hayman making a suggestion that he should visit a particular editor or newspaper and confront them with this intelligence but I do not know what action was taken in this regard.

APPENDIX J

Metropolitan police Authority
Committee Meeting Report 15th September 2011
Partial Transcript

Deputy Commissioner Tim Godwin was asked to answer additional questions from Members.

A Member noted that the MPA had recently hosted the family of Daniel Morgan at a meeting and expressed concerns that the officer investigating their case was subject to surveillance. She asked if there would be an inquiry looking at officers whose phones were hacked and cases they were involved in to see if any information that was relevant at the time of investigation was leaked to the press and whether this prejudiced their cases. She noted that this is a matter of public confidence. Tim Godwin reinforced that the MPS regret the Daniel Morgan case and subsequent investigation. In relation to Dave Cook, he noted that the MPS are exploring that case and as this is part of an ongoing investigation he could not answer any questions on it. He agreed to write to the family in due course and to answer the MPA's questions in writing.

A Member asked what action had been taken by the MPS following Rebekah Brooks' statement to the HASC in 2003 that police officers were being paid for stories, and asked for a response to allegations in the New York Times that the MPS had suppressed inquiries into bribery in order to protect their relationship with NI. Another Member stated that Rebecca Brooks was approached at a press social event and questioned in a side-room by Andrew Baker and Dick Fedorcio regarding surveillance of DCS Cook and no further action was taken. He asked: first, who took the decision to proceed in that way – a conversation with the editor but no further action – and were then Commissioner or Deputy involved or informed? Secondly, were any other senior officers involved or informed? And finally, would John Yate's team who reinvestigated the Daniel Morgan murder have known?

Tim Godwin responded that due to these questions being the subject of ongoing investigation he would have to respond in writing in due course. He noted that the MPS has the most robust anti-corruption command of any police service in England and Wales but when you have 55,000 people on staff, you will always have the odd bad apple.

APPENDIX K

Complete Transcript of Ian Hurst's Witness Statement to the Leveson Inquiry

I, Ian Hurst c/o Collyer Bristow LLP, 4 Bedford Row, London WC1R 4DF will say as follows:

I make this statement in connection with my role as a Core Participant in the Leveson Inquiry.

Background

I am a former member of British Military Intelligence. I served in the Intelligence Corps and Force Research Unit (a covert military intelligence unit) in Northern Ireland between 1980 and 1991. My primary role in Northern Ireland was to recruit and run agents within Republican terrorist groups in order to obtain tactical and strategic intelligence.

I retired from the Army in 1991. My last posting in the Intelligence Corps was for the Defence Intelligence Staff (DIS) of the Ministry of Defence.

In 1997 I decided to write a book. The motivation to write the book was to highlight aspects of my service which had a genuine public interest.

Following a series of articles in The Times in 1999, I was arrested by Special Branch Police officers in connection with alleged offences under the Official Secrets Act. No charges were ever brought against me but I remain subject to an injunction dating back to 1999.

In 2004 I moved with my family to France. During my time in France, I was engaged in researching matters very closely associated with the work I did in Northern Ireland. It is fair to say that I have maintained a close link to the intelligence community since my retirement and I have also come into contact with the workings of the UK and international press on a number of occasions.

Panorama

In the last week of December 2010 I was approached by Stephen Scott, the producer of the BBC Panorama programme. He was making a documentary about the phone and computer hacking scandal that was engulfing News of the World. I attach with this statement a DVD marked "IH1" containing the Panorama documentary that subsequently aired on BBC television in March 2011. I refer to the documentary during the course of this statement.

Mr Scott told me that Panorama had obtained information which showed that I was a potential victim of computer hacking. Mr Scott asked me if I would take part in the Panorama documentary he was making and I readily agreed.

When my wife and I learnt that our computer may have been hacked, we felt it was important to carry out our own investigations to determine whether there was any substance to the claim and we did so during the course of 2011.

Computer hacking revelations

Panorama said it had information which showed that one of our computers had been hacked by News of the World (or at least someone engaged on the paper's behalf) in 2006. During filming, they showed me extracts of emails which had been obtained from my computer and which had been sent by fax to the Dublin office of the News of the World on 5 July of that year marked for the attention of [Alex Marunchak]. I was extremely surprised and concerned by the revelation.

I now know that it is relatively easy for a computer to be 'broken into' and spied on. If a computer is connected to the internet, files and emails on it can be accessed illegally using what is known as a 'Trojan'. This is a piece of software which is usually imbedded in or attached to an email sent to the account of the target individual. Once the email has been opened or the attachment clicked on the Trojan allows the hacker to remotely access and download files such as documents and emails. Effectively the hacker has access to all the information that the computer user does, provided the computer in online.

The hacker

The BBC said they had ascertained that the [editor] of the News of the World [in Ireland] had engaged the private investigator [Jonathan Rees] to target me. [Rees] had then employed a private detective specialising in applying and controlling computer viruses to do the hacking job. The specialist hacker was an individual known to me, having served with him in the intelligence community in Northern Ireland for over 3 years whilst he was attached to the FRU. I will refer to this person [Philip Campbell Smith] as 'X'.

During the making of the Panorama documentary I asked if I could confront X about what I had learnt to allow him to record his position. I initially visited his house but as he was not in I spoke to him on the phone. We arranged to meet at a local hotel straight away. X said he was not surprised that I had made contact as | | had told him two or three days earlier that Panorama were 'sniffing around'. I secretly filmed our meeting and a very small part of it (less than 1 minute from 2 hours of filming) was shown on the Panorama documentary. When the meeting had finished X agreed to let Mr Scott be present for a summary of the points we had talked about.

During the course of our meeting, X stated that he had placed a computer Trojan on my hard drive (by sending me an email from a bogus address which t then opened) and had, over a three month period, obtained all email traffic which was sent and received by me. I now cannot recall whether I opened an email from a bogus address in 2006. However, I can say that I would have been much more likely to have opened an email that had come from a trusted contact rather than an unfamiliar or unknown name. I do know that an email was sent to me by a trusted media contact within Times Newspapers Ltd around the time the Trojan became active and was collecting information from my computer. I have recently seen evidence that this individual was in email contact with X regarding my activities during these months, something which had previously been denied.

X also told me he had attended a meeting in Leeds in mid 2006 with [redacted] and one other News of the World journalist. Apparently X's instructions were to obtain information and documents about activities connected to my ongoing investigations relating to matters in Northern Ireland. X confirmed to me that he had supplied the information obtained from my computer to others involved in the conspiracy.

The News of the World, other newspapers and the Police

I believe that News of the World employees targeted me for a number of reasons and certainly because of my work in Northern Ireland and the investigations I have been involved in since my service. I think they may have been trying to obtain information on an IRA informer with the code name [Stakeknife]. During 2006 I was investigating the possibility of bringing a private prosecution or claim for defamation claim against [redacted] I have seen evidence that emails between me and Carter Ruck (which were legally privileged) and information exchanged between me and Jane Winter of the British Irish Rights Watch were intercepted by X.

After I was made aware of the hacking of my own computer I starting looking into the practice in general. I am convinced that computer hacking was not confined to the News of the World and there were other newspapers engaged in this type of illegal information gathering. I am also absolutely certain that there were strong links between certain newspapers and former and current officers of the Metropolitan Police Service.

The police have admitted to me that documents and hardware seized in 2007 during the arrest of [redacted] showed that the security of my computer had been compromised and information had been obtained from it. This position was reinforced by the arrest of X during 2009 when further information was obtained from his seized computers. Even though the police were aware that my computer had been hacked as long ago as 2007, they did not inform me until October of this year. I strongly feel that the matter was 'swept under the carpet' and if the hacking had been fully investigated by the police when it first came to light further illegal information gathering would not have occurred. I am now bringing a civil claim in relation to the hacking of my computer.

Following the filming of the Panorama documentary, I have uncovered a considerable amount of evidence about the unhealthy role played by the police. I will be providing a further, more detailed statement for Part 2 of the Inquiry.

APPENDIX L

Theresa May's Written Statement to Parliament, 10th May 2013

The Secretary of State for the Home Department (Theresa May):

Daniel Morgan, a private investigator, was found murdered in a pub car park in south east London on 10 March 1987. It is one of the country's most notorious unsolved murder cases. After numerous separate police investigations into the case between 1987 and 2002, the Crown Prosecution Service discontinued the final attempted prosecution against five suspects in 2011.

The Metropolitan Police (MPS) have indicated that there is no likelihood of any successful prosecutions being brought in the foreseeable future. They have also admitted that police corruption was a "debilitating factor" in the original investigation. This has led to calls for an inquiry from Mr Morgan's family, who have waged a long campaign for those responsible for his murder to be brought to justice. I have met with the family and, after further serious consideration with them and their representatives, I am today announcing the creation of the Daniel Morgan Independent Panel.

Importantly, the Panel's work will put Mr Morgan's family at the centre of the process and the approach to this issue has the support of the MPS Commissioner and the Independent Police Complaints Commission.

The Panel will utilise learning from the Hillsborough Independent Panel process in addressing how to approach its work. The Panel will be chaired by Sir Stanley Burnton, a retired Lord Justice of the Court of Appeal. The appointment of other members of the Panel will take place over the coming weeks and will be announced as soon as possible.

The remit of the Panel will be to shine a light on the circumstances of Daniel Morgan's murder, its background and the handling of the case over the period since 1987. In doing so, the Panel will seek to address the questions arising, including those relating to:

- police involvement in the murder;
- the role played by police corruption in protecting those responsible for the murder from being brought to justice and the failure to confront that corruption;
- the incidence of connections between private investigators, police officers and journalists at the News of the World and other parts of the media and alleged corruption involved in the linkages between them.

The Panel will ensure maximum possible disclosure of all relevant documentation, including information held by all relevant Government departments and agencies and by the police and other investigative and prosecuting authorities. There is a serious and considerable public interest in having an independent panel look at this case, as part of the Government's commitment to identifying, exposing and addressing corruption.

Recognising the volume of material that must be catalogued, analysed and preserved, the Panel will seek to complete its work within a year of the documentation being made available.

A copy of the full terms of reference of the Daniel Morgan Independent Panel has been placed in the Library of the House.